MEENA,
HEROINE OF AFGHANISTAN

Also by Melody Ermachild Chavis

Altars in the Street:
A Courageous Memoir of Community
and Spiritual Awakening

For Claire,

MEENA,
HEROINE OF AFGHANISTAN

The Martyr
Who Founded
RAWA, the
Revolutionary
Association of
the Women
of Afghanistan

...another Meena!

Melody Ermachild Chavis

Melody Ermachild Chavis
Foreword by Alice Walker

ST. MARTIN'S PRESS ❧ NEW YORK

www.stmartins.com

Meena's poetry reprinted here courtesy of RAWA.

"Meena Lives Within Us" by Neesha Mirchandani reprinted here by permission of the author.

Photographs, except for p. 38, courtesy of RAWA.

Library of Congress Cataloging-in-Publication Data

Chavis, Melody Ermachild.
    Meena, heroine of Afghanistan : the martyr who founded RAWA, the
Revolutionary Association of the Women of Afghanistan / Melody Ermachild Chavis ;
with a foreword by Alice Walker.
      p. cm.
    ISBN 0-312-30689-X
    1. Meena, 1937-1987.   2. Women social reformers—Afghanistan—Biography.
3. Revolutionary Association of the Women of Afghanistan—History.   I. Title.
HQ1735.6.Z75M443 2003
303.484'092—dc21

                                          200300295

First Edition: August 2003

10 9 8 7 6 5 4 3 2 1

This book is for
the young Meenas of this world
who will grow up to fight against
injustice and fundamentalism,
and carry on the struggle for
peace, freedom, democracy,
and women's rights.

CONTENTS

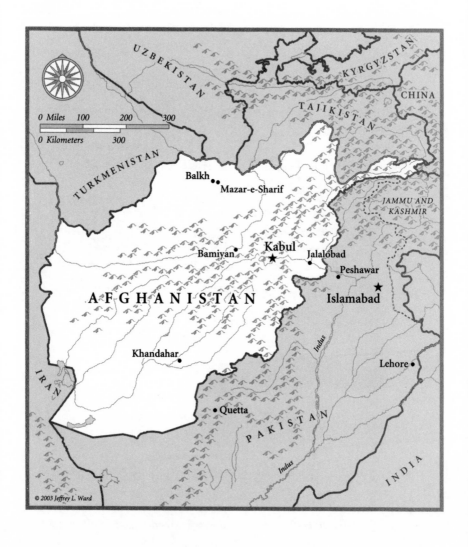

© 2003 Jeffrey L. Ward

FOREWORD

Alice Walker

As life would have it, the same week I received the manuscript of Meena's life, I finished reading a memoir, *Walking Through Fire* by the great African-Egyptian writer Nawal El Saadawi. My mind was completely open to the vast difficulties that Islamic fundamentalism presents to millions of women around the globe. Saadawi's un-schooled, severely oppressed mother had had only a few words to give her daughter to strengthen her as she encountered challenges the women of her mother's generation never dreamed. She said of Nawal: "Throw her into a fire and she will come out unscathed. There never was a more clever person than Nawal." These few words would come back again and again in Saadawi's life: when she was treated with disdain as she studied to become a doctor; when she was married off to a man she did not love; when she was arrested by her government because she criticized its policies; when her name was placed on a death list and she was forced to flee her country; when she began to create a new life, at over sixty years of age, in a new country.

I am humbled by the gifts our parents give us, sometimes un-knowingly. It is the praise of us that encourages us; the seeing of us. That we are worthy and precious in their sight. Sometimes a word is all a parent can give a child, the oppression all around is so intense. As it became under the rule of the Taliban in Afghan-istan.

Meena's father named her Meena because in Farsi, their native language, it means "light." She was a bright, black-haired, black-eyed girl who loved to run about gleefully, playing with her siblings, well loved by her two mothers and especially by her father, who called her his "heart." When she was stricken with typhoid at the age of twelve the whole family grieved, fearful she might die. After an agonizing illness, Meena recovered, though she remained somewhat delicate and plagued with seizures when stressed. I believe it was this illness, however, that set her apart and began to reveal to her both the suffering of women in her society and her own gift, which was compassion and love. And a boldness of imagination often felt by those who have escaped death early in life. Meena seems never to have doubted that the horrid situation women endured in her society might be changed. Or that she, one small Afghan woman, walking among her people literally wearing a shroud, the so-called *burqa*, might dare to begin this awesome task.

This is a story the world must learn by heart. For Afghanistan clearly demonstrates our future as a planet if we do not immediately make the decision to honor the feminine. *Meena* lays bare the futility of war; the inanity of forced illiteracy; the self-destructiveness of woman-hating. How does anyone expect to survive while denigrating and degrading one-half of the self? It could not be clearer, reading this story of a hero and a goddess, that by killing off the one who cares for the children, the one who champions the oppressed, the one who tends the wounded and the sick, the one who feeds the hungry, the one who shelters the poor, the one who dances and laughs, the one who objects to injustice ceaselessly, a society turns itself into a land of the treacherous, the uncaring, and the dead.

After founding, with a few other trusted women, *Jamiat Zan Inkalab Afghanistan*, the Revolutionary Association of the Women of Afghanistan, Meena devoted her life to the liberation of Afghan women, and to the health and freedom of the entire Afghan people. This story gives us insight into how a small group of determined, compassionate, and courageous women, led by the "light" that was Meena, kept alive in the hearts of millions of their people—during a time of unimaginable darkness—the idea that they were seen; they were believed in; they were precious and beloved, after all.

Meena, having bravely taken word of her people's desperate plight to the ears of the world, and having accepted exile as the price for doing so, continued her endless work to help her war-devoured country. Her last project was the building and staffing of a hospital that would treat the thousands of Afghans injured by land mines. She was assassinated by someone she knew, someone she trusted. Someone who smiled at the feminine force that took him in and honored him, but could not refrain from envying and extinguishing her light. And yet, how prophetic her father's naming of her was. Though murdered, her light remained unshrouded. Her love for all those she helped in life was the light that led them to her hidden grave.

Women of the world and men who love us, such a woman as Meena must not have died in vain. Honor the feminine in all things. It is that which connects us to Life, and is its beat. It is separate from nothing, and therefore cannot be put aside without grave danger to everything.

One day one hopes the whole of Afghanistan, healed after so many centuries of war, will look upon the smiling, radiant face of Meena and recognize itself. Under the illusion that she is separate from them, the male leaders of Afghanistan cannot see her today, to their loss, though women of Afghanistan keep photographs of her close to their hearts. Shrouding women's bodies, men have covered over their own vision and intelligence. Their own connection to the divine. When I think of this young woman, her husband murdered, herself dead at the age of thirty, their children left orphaned, I realize how great is the human capacity for loving kindness, for compassion, for grace. A woman with a price on her head, always needing to travel with bodyguards, a woman severely overworked and not in perfect health, a woman who often had to walk through dangerous territory to get where she was going, Meena, nonetheless, was famous for being punctual, for showing up on time. She understood that people—women, children, the sick and oppressed—depended on her. Perhaps this is her final message to us as we face danger and uncertainty in the world: Dare to show up. Dare to be punctual. Dare to be present in your time. Above all, dare to offer the word of praise and delight that encourages the heart. All the world is connected by breath and this is the road traveled by words. It will never be completely blocked.

Long live Meena. And long live the freedom (it is coming) of women in Afghanistan. And long live the freedom, too (it is coming), of men in Afghanistan.

MEENA,
HEROINE OF AFGHANISTAN

1

A GIRL BETWEEN
THE OLD WORLD
AND THE NEW

Meena lay on the *toshak*, the big cushion on the floor of her family's sleeping room, only half-conscious of her mother's hands stroking her thick dark hair. Her father, too, knelt beside her on the ruby red carpet, bathing her hot face with a cool, wet cloth. Her fever had reached 105 degrees. She was drenched in sweat, but she shivered as if she were freezing. It was a hot day, yet she could not get warm no matter how many quilts her mother placed over her.

Meena's brothers and sisters took turns peering anxiously from the doorway. Meena moaned and tried to turn over. The younger children could hardly believe that the thin form, lying almost invisible under the thick pile of quilts, was their big sister Meena. She was usually lively and talkative. She was rebellious, too, and ran and screamed with them and made as much noise as she could until their parents told her to be quiet. Sometimes, she was so opinionated and even bossy, that she seemed like their second mother. Now she was so weak that she looked younger than her twelve years.

Meena knew her illness must be very contagious, because her little sisters and brothers were not allowed to come into the room. She longed to hug them and feel their sweet little bodies close to hers. Usually in the summer, the sleeping cushions were moved outside into the courtyard, where the whole family enjoyed sleeping

The earliest-known
photo of Meena, found
in Kabul after the Taliban
relinquished the
city in 2002.

together under a big summer tent of mosquito netting. But now
Meena lay inside, with only her frantic parents nearby.

Her father had named her Meena, the Farsi word for "Light."
He often said, "She is the light of my life," and he loved to call her
"my heart." From the time she was born, she had been his special
child, intelligent and sweet-natured, and he had wanted the best
for her. Meena's whole family had loved her mischievous smile and
her easy laugh. And they all remarked on her bright eyes, black as
coal. Now her eyes were closed, and her round cheeks were hot
and dry to the touch.

Meena had fallen ill a week before. At first she had been sick to
her stomach and lost her appetite. Meal after meal she took only a
few small bites of her mother's *naan*—the big flat loaves of un-
leavened bread Meena usually loved. Then the morning came when
Meena could not get out of bed. Crying, she told her mother that

she saw white spots—pieces of light that got larger until she could no longer see. Then she fainted. Now, she was not speaking at all.

Because Meena's father, Latif, was an architect, often employed by the government of the Afghan king, her family had enough money to send for a doctor. The diagnosis was typhoid fever, common in Afghanistan in 1969. At least one-fourth of the victims died. Even in their city of Kabul, drinking water was not always safe, typhoid was common, and medicines were scarce.

If Meena had lived in Europe, she would have been in a modern hospital, hooked to an intravenous tube delivering antibiotics to her fevered body. Had she lived out in the Afghan countryside far from the capital, she probably would have died without any treatment at all.

At twelve, Meena was old enough to realize, after the doctor's visit, that she might not recover. Her mother's tears and her father's sad face told her so. Meena had known other children who had died of diseases, even some in her large extended family. As she slipped into unconsciousness, she wondered if she were dying, but she felt too weak and cold to resist.

She had been born at home, in 1957, in this very room. When the Muslim priest, the Mullah, came to bless her birth, he pronounced: "She will be a queen, but she will not live to old age." The Mullah's words seemed to doom her now.

Suddenly, Meena went rigid. Her chin trembled, and her face contorted. Her spine arched off the cushions, and her head jerked back. She was having a seizure caused by her fever.

There was nothing Meena's parents could do except hold and stroke her. It subsided a minute later. Her parents were terrified that even if she lived, the seizures might permanently damage her brain. The loss of Meena's sparkling intelligence would be a tragedy they would not be able to bear.

As a baby, she had talked even before she had walked. Once she learned to talk, her parents often joked, she had never stopped. Her favorite thing was to follow adults around, asking them questions.

She learned to read easily, and had done so well in school that she had passed the exams for entry into the best high school for girls in Afghanistan. She was to have the rarest gift for an Afghan girl: an excellent education.

Now, her parents waited through the night, sitting anxiously beside her, hoping the medicine prescribed by the doctor would work. They had to face the possibility that perhaps their Meena was among the unluckiest Afghan children after all—one of the countless youngsters who died before anyone knew what they might do with their lives. Meena lay still, barely seeming to breathe.

At last, toward morning, Meena's fever broke. The danger passed, but she was left so weak she could not walk. At first, light from the window was too bright for her eyes. She slept for days in the darkened room, hardy believing that she was still alive. The ordinary sounds of her neighborhood—the squeaking wheels of wooden hand carts called karachis, the clopping of horses' feet in the street outside, the engines of cars and buses passing, the talk and laughter of the neighbors in their courtyards—pierced her ears. Only the songs of the birds in her family's fruit trees comforted her.

Meena's father carried her to a chair outside, where she could see the high folded peaks of the mountains rising above the Kabul River. Meena usually loved to go out into the busy city. Now she wanted only to stay behind the walls that enclosed her family's home and gaze quietly at the grey-and-purple mountains that sometimes seemed close enough to touch.

Meena's father, Latif, came from a family who had lived in the city of Kabul for two generations. Their home was in an old hillside neighborhood called Kartai-Parwan, where families lived who were neither rich nor poor. Many were teachers, government workers, or professionals like Latif. He had gone to Istiqlal High School in Kabul and then to technical college, where he studied architecture. He designed government buildings, and also private homes. Latif was clever and resourceful. He was famous in the family for being able to build or fix anything. He loved maps, and he also worked on preparing official maps of Afghanistan.

Meena's people were ethnic Pashtuns, the majority group in Afghanistan, and the tribe of the kings who had ruled the nation for more than two hundred years. Meena's strong features—her definite forehead, nose, and chin, and her dark eyes and hair—are typical Pashtun physical traits, easily recognized among the many tribes of Afghanistan.

For all of Meena's twelve years, Afghanistan had been at peace. Her country was a place where diverse peoples lived side by side in relative harmony, and hardship. To Afghans, hospitality is the highest duty. Even starving villagers, facing famine brought on by poor crops, would offer guests a bowl of hot boiled grass, even if that was all they had to eat.

Meena's family, like their neighbors, lived in privacy inside their enclosed compound. High brown mud or stone walls lined the narrow dusty streets in their part of the city. Behind the walls, families lived in an intimate world of their own. The family had several common rooms for living. There were separate cooking and laundry rooms and storehouses for supplies, all arranged around the central courtyard with trees and plants. Nearly all city families kept chickens, and some even had goats. Well-off families also had rooms for servants. No one had individual private rooms, and each member of the family had only a few personal possessions.

At mealtime, Meena and the other children were told, "Go and wash your hands." Then everyone gathered around a colorful *destarkhan*, a cloth spread on the floor. They sat close together, using their hands and pieces of *naan* to scoop rice mixed with nuts and raisins and pieces of roasted chicken from big bowls. Everyone watched what Meena ate, and tried to tempt her to eat more, hoping she would gain back some of the weight she had lost while she was sick. Meena's family of ten children was not at all unusual in Kabul. Often, aunts, uncles, and cousins were seated around the *destarkhan* also. Everyone talked and laughed, and at Meena's favorite times, the *robab* would come out, a stringed instrument, and small drums, and everyone would sing. Usually, Meena hated to go to bed. She loved to be allowed to lie down near the grown-ups and fall asleep listening to their talk and laughter. But after she had been sick with typhoid, she fell asleep right away.

At night, the *toshak* cushions along the walls were pulled out into the middle of the rooms and became the family's beds, where they slept side by side. Family members enjoyed being together, and hardly anyone was ever alone.

The women in Afghan families spent most of their time with each other. Each morning and evening, women carrying bundles walked in groups to the *hamom*, the neighborhood baths, where water for washing was heated communally. There the women bathed together and had a chance to visit. The women's support for each other was so essential to their lives that a woman without her mother, mother-in-law, sisters, aunts, and female cousins living close by was very much pitied.

Afghan tradition required modesty in women. Meena's mothers and aunts wore long skirts and scarves covering their hair when they went out, as most Kabul women did. A guest room near the front door of each house allowed the men of the house to entertain male visitors. This left the inner rooms free for the women to live without fear of being seen by men who were not relatives.

The lives of women in the countryside were harsher and more restricted than in the cities. In the most traditional and religious villages, most women wore a head-to-toe covering—a *burqa*, which covers the face and forces the wearer to try to see where she is going through a mesh over the eyes. The *burqa* was becoming less popular when Meena was a girl. Women seen wearing it in the city were assumed to be visiting from the countryside.

Most city families had relatives in rural villages, where they returned for important occasions like weddings and funerals. Much of the food city people ate came from the farms of their country relatives. Over centuries, Afghan farmers had learned how to grow wheat in the dry, thin soil of the fragile mountain valleys, watered by rainfall or streams. At lower, warmer elevations, rice was grown in emerald green paddies. Lower still, people kept camels that grazed among date palm trees. Families of nomads roamed hundreds of miles across the countryside, herding sheep and goats. Villagers used the wool of their animals to weave carpets. This was the ancient Afghan culture that had persisted unaltered for centuries. The fact that it resisted change was both its beauty and its curse.

When Meena's family traveled to visit their relatives, she often saw people who were too poor even to afford a draft animal to help them plow the fields. It was a common sight to see a man behind a plow, wrestling the wooden handles, pushing the blade through the tough ground, while the woman walked in front, bent over, pulling the plow forward with a rope—a technology thousands of years old.

The vast majority of Afghan men and women were illiterate farmers who did hard labor in the fields. Life went along as it had for centuries, not only because of the lack of modern technology, but because the wisdom of the past had ensured the tenuous survival of people. To peasants, it was obvious that science did not bring food; they depended on God's grace to send rainfall to water the crops in this harsh and fragile land.

On buses crossing the countryside, men were given the seats inside. Women rode on top of the bus, clinging to the baggage, even in burning hot sun, rain, or blowing dust. Meena once saw a bus stopped along the roadside with a desperately ill woman lying on the baggage. Her husband was handing tea and bread up to her, but she was too weak to take it. She was trying to get to Kabul, where there was a hospital and medicines.

Meena started to cry. "What is the matter?" her mother, Hanifa, asked her.

"Why does she have to ride in the heat?" Meena asked through her tears. "She's so sick. Why can't she ride inside?"

"Come here, Meena," her mother said, taking her onto her lap and patting her. "I know it's terrible," Hanifa said, "but there's nothing we can do."

Quietly and sadly she added, "It's probably the least of what she has to suffer."

In old-fashioned village families, men were valued so much more than women that the birth of a baby girl was greeted with sorrow. Mothers of newborn girls were offered sympathy if they were lucky; unlucky ones were blamed and even divorced.

Though they lived in the city, Meena's family had strong ties to village traditions. Her grandmother, mother, and aunts lived with those ancient rules. The fact that they could not read hardly mattered. A woman like Meena's mother, Hanifa, an accomplished mother of ten, knew all she needed to know—according to tradition—to run her household. She knew many prayers and poems by heart, but she would never read a newspaper or a book. It was not unusual in Afghanistan for an educated man like Latif to be married to a woman who, like Hanifa, had never gone to school. Hanifa was an intelligent woman who was interested in the modern world. Though she could not read herself, she wanted her daughters to be as well educated as her sons, and Meena's father, Latif, agreed.

In Afghan tradition, many men had more than one wife. Muslim law allows up to four. This custom was dying out among urban families, but many still followed the older ways. Latif's first wife was the mother of Meena's two teenage brothers. Latif had then married his second wife, Hanifa. Meena was the oldest of Hanifa's children, and the oldest girl in the family. Between them, Latif's two wives had ten children.

Meena loved both her mother and her stepmother very much, having known them both all her life. She admired her mothers for the way they loved all of their children and cared for their home together to make it a happy place for everyone. People said they could hardly tell which one was Meena's real mother because Meena was so close to both of them.

To help her recover from typhoid, Meena's mothers brought her pomegranates to eat, red jewel-like fruits that came from the fertile valleys outside Kabul. Their lumpy oval shape reminded Meena of the map of Afghanistan, called "The Heart of Asia." Slowly, she gained strength.

Recuperating from typhoid fever in her family home, Meena was surrounded by the close circle of her parents and brothers and sisters. She also was a member of a much larger extended family. Her many aunts, uncles, and cousins thought of her not as Meena, one little girl, but Meena descended from generations of Afghans and was born into the place where she belonged, part of a clan with its own passed-down stories and traditions. The most favored marriages for Afghans were between cousins. This meant that the big clanlike families curled in on themselves, with many members sharing grandparents and great-grandparents, so that ties were very close. The big family provided security for everyone in it—if people died or were ill, if they needed money or food, each member could turn to the others for help.

The sound of the voice of the *azzan*, the priest at the mosque, calling the faithful to prayer five times a day, sounded to Meena like a gentle call back to life. Islam was like a familiar embrace to her.

There are as many forms of Islam as there are nations and peoples who practice it. For the majority of Afghans, religion was a soft thread in the fabric of life. The calls to prayer were part of each day's rhythm; people stopped to pray, or not, as they wished. The Mullahs—priests who ran the mosques and taught in the religious schools, had influence, but they were not the government. Islam was so much a part of life in Afghanistan that it was like the air. It so permeated everything that it was almost invisible.

As she gradually realized that she would live, Meena wondered why. She was a romantic and earnest person. To her, it seemed that her life must have been spared for some purpose greater than the ordinary fate of an Afghan girl. Meena had already done something neither her mother nor her grandmother had done: She had gone to school. She was part of a new generation of young women, unlike any that Afghanistan had ever seen.

In some ways, Afghanistan was just entering the age of print. Books and newspapers were common only in the cities. In the villages, news was brought by word of mouth, and storytelling was the entertainment. Afghan culture was an oral tradition, in which poetry, songs, and stories were passed down through generations and valued more than books. Only about 10 percent of Afghans were able to read and write.

Meena had loved school from the start. She was such a good student that her parents wanted her to go to Kabul University. She could take up a career among the small but growing group of professional Afghan women who practiced medicine and law and taught school. Meena was poised at the edge of a new world. Yet her future was uncertain because the old world exerted its strong pull on her.

At twelve, Meena was already at an age when many Afghan girls had their marriages arranged. Most girls still married young and left school before they finished. As the oldest girl in a family of ten children, Meena knew what housework was. As soon as she was big enough, one of her mothers would say, "Meena, the baby is crying. Go and pick him up." Meena helped to pat out the bread dough before school, and she swept the courtyard when she got home in the afternoons. Meena was a good eldest daughter and big sister. She learned to put the needs of the younger children ahead of her own. She was so responsible that she learned to offer them food, or change their diapers, or pick them up and rock them even before they began to cry.

But sometimes Meena felt she would rather die than spend her life confined in the house like her mothers and her grandmother. There had to be more to life than preparing meals, cleaning, and answering the endless demands of children. She was determined to do something more with her life. She wanted to have the same chances as her brothers to have a career, to see other places, to have people listen to her ideas.

Reading was Meena's way of escaping and of dreaming of the future she hoped to have. She spent the weeks when she was still too weak to go to school dozing in the shade and reading. Her favorite novels were by the American adventurer and rebel Jack London, whose books had been translated into many languages, including Farsi. London wrote about the wretched lives of slaves and poor workers. He exposed the cruelty of plantation overseers and factory owners in the early years of capitalism. His novels about injustice and his exciting adventure stories were enormously popular in Afghanistan. Engrossed in *The Call of the Wild*, Meena was no longer in Kabul, but in faraway Alaska. She longed to see the world, but it seemed to her that only men were allowed to have adventures like Jack London's heroes, mushing across the tundra, sailing the stormy seas, and fighting for justice.

Typhoid fever changed Meena. She never regained her full strength. Her legs ached when she got cold, or if she walked too far. Worst of all, she was left with epilepsy. When she became too tired or upset, she sometimes collapsed in a seizure like the one she had at the height of her fever.

Meena's illness had changed her in other ways, too. The first twelve years of her life had been filled with love. She was a beautiful girl with striking features: large black eyes framed by arched brows, a high forehead and strong chin defining her sweet, rounded face, and thick, long dark hair. Everyone who looked at her smiled, and she had smiled back at the world. Her grandmother and her aunts and uncles had always spoiled her with little gifts and treats. When her favorite uncle came to visit she would run to him, and demand, "What do you have for me in your pockets?" as he scooped her up in a big hug.

Now, she was a more serious person, changed from a little girl to a young woman in the space of a few desperate weeks fighting for her life. She had a new look in her eyes, as if a slight shadow had fallen across her gaze. As strength gradually flowed back into her body, so did a resolve to use her second chance at life for a purpose larger than herself.

2

A TEENAGER IN KABUL

At last Meena was strong enough to return to school. Each morning she joined the other high-spirited girls crowded into one of the electric buses that lumbered along Kabul's broad, landscaped avenues on the way to school. The bus stopped in front of the long white stucco wall that enclosed Malalai Girls High School. The girls, all dressed in black dresses over black stockings, their heads covered with white scarves, giggled and pushed as they lined up in the park that surrounded the large three-story white buildings. The seniors, tall teenagers, stood at the front of the lines, keeping order. Each morning, the principal came out to greet her students. Everyone saluted the black, green, and white Afghan flag before the girls followed their teachers to class.

The whole Malalai community was extremely proud because their school was named for the most famous Afghan woman. The real Malalai was a national heroine of the Afghan war of liberation. In the summer of 1880, the British, who had conquered India, attempted to extend their rule over Afghanistan, and the Afghans fought back. At the Battle of Maiwand, the Afghans were taking a terrible beating from British guns. Behind the line of fire, Afghan women were encamped, supplying their husbands and brothers with water, food, and bandages.

Nearly all of the Afghan fighters were killed. They simply did not have the guns the British had. The few remaining Afghan men

Meena as a schoolgirl.

ran back in terror, fleeing a British charge. Their flag bearer was hit and as he fell, he dropped the Afghan flag.

Malalai, whose husband and brothers were in the battle, ran forward and seized the flag. She stood firmly in the midst of bursting shells, holding the flag high. She turned to shout to the retreating men.

Though Malalai was illiterate, she knew the traditional poetry of her proud culture. *Jandei*, ancient tribal chanted poems, were to her like breathing or singing. On the spot, Malalai made up a *Jandei* and sang it out:

> With a drop of my sweetheart's blood
> shed in defense of the Motherland
> will I put a beauty spot on my face
> such as would put to shame the rose in the garden.
> If you come back alive from the Battle of Maiwand,
> I swear, my sweetheart, that the rest of your days
> you will live in shame.

As Malalai's song died from her lips, she was shot down and killed. Inspired by her example, the Afghan men returned and won the battle.

In 1919, as soon as Afghanistan won its final independence from the British, the Afghan king, Amanullah Khan, set about modernizing the country. He invited French and German educators to set up European-style schools for girls in 1921. Meena's school was established by French teachers, which is why the brass plate beside the iron front gate read: LYCÉE MALALAI. *Lycée* is French for high school. The girls addressed the teachers as "Madame."

By the 1960s, when Meena was at Malalai, her teachers were modern working women. Their uniforms were green dresses with calf-length skirts. Meena's teachers wore makeup, jewelry, and attractive hairstyles. Some modestly covered their heads with scarves, some chose not to; both religious practice and dress were considered personal decisions. The school was disciplined, and proper behavior was expected of the girls, but it was modern. Girls were taught the same subjects boys learned in their schools. They went to school all morning, taking six subjects each day before they went home for a midday meal.

History was Meena's favorite subject, and her favorite teacher taught it. Madame Nooria was a short, energetic woman in her forties, a passionate lecturer determined to engage the minds of her students. Her class met in one of Malalai's high-ceilinged classrooms, bright with white walls and high windows looking out into the tall trees.

From Madame Nooria, Meena learned that if she had been born even twenty years earlier, her chance for an education would have been almost nil. During Meena's whole childhood, Afghanistan had been at peace, in a period which many people called the "Royal Democracy." Afghanistan was ruled by a benevolent if somewhat neglectful monarch, King Zahir. The king was a lover of modern ideas and of European culture, which he brought back from his many trips abroad. He appointed his relatives to all of the important government posts, and for months at a time they ran the country while he vacationed in France.

Before Meena was old enough to go to school, King Zahir had

made Kabul University coeducational. Rapidly, women enrolled and entered the workforce. The king used his power to help women to work outside their homes by first offering them government jobs. On the official station, Radio Afghanistan, women's voices were heard reading the news. At first there were protests, but slowly female newscasters were accepted. Women worked also at the national airline, Ariana, and as telephone operators and factory workers. They worked unveiled, as cumbersome clothing would have impeded headsets and machinery. Slowly, these changes were accepted.

In 1963, when Meena was six, King Zahir fired the prime minister, his cousin Sardar Daoud, who had served for ten years. Daoud had aligned Afghanistan more closely to the Soviet Union, its neighbor to the north, inviting in Russian advisors and sending young Afghans to study at Soviet universities. The king disagreed with Daoud's pro-Soviet views, fired him, and pushed the country in a more Western-oriented, liberal direction.

In 1964, King Zahir convened a national Grand Council, called a *Loya Jirga* in the Pashtun language. The *Loya Jirga* is a semidemocratic tribal tradition. For centuries, kings had been chosen by this method. Councils of elders called *Shuras* met in each village. Unfortunately, the *Shuras* represented only the wealthiest families in each region, not the ordinary people like Meena's family. The voices of women, minorities, and poor people were not heard. The *Shuras* chose delegates. These delegates, sometimes a total of two thousand powerful men, traveled to the capital for the *Loya Jirga*.

Madame Nooria explained that in 1964, when Meena and her classmates were only six or seven, women took part in the *Loya Jirga* for the first time in history. They were not full delegates, but the king appointed six women to an advisory committee that was drafting a new constitution for the nation. The women pushed for the right to vote. With the king's support, the vote was granted to both women and men.

Both of Meena's parents voted, for the first time in their lives, in September, 1965, in the first-ever nationwide elections for a parliament. The king retained much more than ceremonial powers, but Afghanistan was moving closer to something like a European-style constitutional monarchy. The new constitution also allowed for more freedom of speech and the press.

To Meena, the history she learned from Madame Nooria was not abstract. Her father had a well-paid, modern government job. For city people like her parents, the changes the king had made when she was younger were positive. Kabul was the intellectual center of the country, its 350,000 people bustling among new buildings and highways being built. The university was growing, and many technical and high schools. Thousands of foreigners had come to teach. The modern airport was served by several airlines. There were restaurants and theaters.

Meena's family visited the zoo, took picnics to the shrines on the hillsides, and walked in the lovely city parks, filled with flowers and trees. Colorful kites flew everywhere, because making kites and flying them was a popular Afghan hobby. Near the center of the city there was a park set aside for women, where they could relax together without being approached by men.

Best of all, to Meena, was the museum, which had one of the most famous archeological collections in the world, with priceless antiquities from the many empires that had conquered Afghanistan over centuries. There were Greek and Roman artifacts, Moghul and Mongol treasures, including enchanting glass objects two thousand years old.

Meena's parents expected each one of their children, including their five daughters, to go to high school and have bright futures. In spite of her seizures and aching legs from typhoid, Meena was determined to live up to her parents' hopes. She had her own goals and dreams, and she excelled at school. Meena's father was proud of her achievements. He often urged her, Study hard, so that you can grow up to help our country.

Meena's history teacher, Madame Nooria, also encouraged the girls to debate the burning issues confronting Afghanistan. For their generation, the greatest moral challenge was the inequality they saw every day around them. Life for the educated minority in the cities was so much better than life for villagers subsisting from share-cropping that progress in Afghanistan was a crucial moral issue.

Madame Nooria showed the girls statistics that proved that Afghanistan was one of the very few nations on earth where women lived shorter lives than men. This was because boys and men were often fed before girls and women. When food was scarce, that could mean malnutrition or even starvation for women. There was so little access to medical care that women died in childbirth, and young children died of disease more often than anywhere else on earth.

Many of the new intellectuals were determined to do something to help the rural people who had no access to education or health care. Madame Nooria challenged her students: "Well-off young women like you should not be complacent about your privileges. You have a duty to reach out to help villagers to better themselves also."

Madame Nooria told her students, "It's not enough to offer only charity. What good will it do to feed a few starving people when the unfair system of land ownership keeps the poor farmers so close to famine all the time?"

Meena's sense of justice and fairness was outraged by the fate of poor women in Afghanistan. She promised herself and her teacher that she would work to make changes that would give the peasants, especially peasant women, better lives.

But if Afghans wanted to change the system, how should they do that? What form of government and land ownership could replace the king and feudal lords? Madame Nooria impressed on her students that they bore a heavy responsibility. All over the world, monarchies were falling. Small groups of educated people, sometimes even students, had sparked revolutions that swept away one system and replaced it with another, seemingly overnight.

Afghanistan was geographically very far away from any democratic nation. Europe and America seemed to exist in a different universe. Still, Madame Nooria taught the girls about the United

States Constitution and the American right to life, liberty, and the pursuit of happiness. She taught them about the French Revolution for Liberty, Fraternity, and Equality. She lectured on the evils of despotism in the whole world. She introduced the principles of democracy and women's rights. Most of all, she taught the girls that all good citizens had a duty to rebel against tyranny.

Though Madame Nooria taught her students to admire Western democracy, she also warned them not to trust the West, which had plundered the Muslim world in the past. Britain had taken India, Napoleon Bonaparte of France had tried to take Egypt and Syria, Britain and Russia had divided up Iran, and France had taken Algeria, Morocco, and Tunisia. After World War I, Britain and France had taken over Syria, Lebanon, Palestine, and Iraq. When Indians finally won their independence from Britain in 1947, after generations of struggle, Britain had partitioned India and created Pakistan, over the objections of Mahatma Gandhi and the Muslim nonviolent leader Badshah Khan, who wanted Hindus and Muslims to share India in peace.

Still, many educated Afghans, like most of Malalai's teachers, readily adopted Western science and modern democratic ways, and wanted to meld them with Afghan traditions. Madame Nooria believed that the education of a new generation was the way to accomplish this. To her mind, Afghan culture could accommodate democracy, tolerance, and human rights, but only if Afghanistan could take the time to set its own agenda and modernize at its own pace. But time was running out.

Afghanistan was surrounded on all sides by other poverty-stricken Muslim nations undergoing rapid change, each one with a different approach: In Iraq and Egypt, for example, army officers had expelled the royal families and set up military dictatorships.

Next door in Iran, the United States had helped overthrow an anti-American elected government and installed Shah Reza Pahlavi, who ruled with an iron hand. Iranians had no freedom of speech or of the press. Any kind of opposition to the autocratic rule of the shah resulted in imprisonment, and very often torture and execution. The Shah's royal family flaunted their fabulous wealth while oppressing the Iranian people with their brutal secret police, the SAVAK.

Madame Nooria loaned Meena one of her own favorite books: *The Epic of Resistance*, a memoir by an Iranian woman, Ashraf Dihquany. Ashraf was a freedom fighter who was savagely tortured while imprisoned in Iran for her activities against the Shah. Like most teenagers, Meena was alert to adult hypocrisy. She admired U.S.-style democracy, but the example of the Shah's regime made democracy-minded students like Meena suspicious of the intentions of America.

Meena was not at all shy. Her hand was always raised in class, with a question or an answer. In Madame Nooria, Meena had found the perfect mentor, a woman whose passions matched hers. It was Madame Nooria who instilled a hatred of injustice in Meena.

Even in her literature class, which she also loved, Meena's questioning mind found rich food for political thought. The girls learned about the life of the Afghan woman poet, Rabia Balkhi, for whom another girls' school in Kabul was named. Rabia had lived in the tenth century, in the ancient northern Afghan kingdom of Balkh. She fell in love with a Turkish slave and wrote passionate love poems to him. When her brother discovered the poems, he murdered her. He ordered Rabia's wrists slashed before she was thrown into a steam bath. According to the legend, she wrote a poem to her lover on the wall, with the last of her blood.

Malalai and Rabia Balkhi are both revered by Afghan men and women, but the lesson of their tales seemed to be: If an Afghan woman steps outside of her traditional role—if she becomes a freedom fighter or a passionate lover and poet—her fate will be a tragic, if heroic, death. She might be honored after she is dead for fighting the enemy or for writing poetry and loving passionately, but no living woman would be.

Meena admired these women and wanted to emulate them, but

like many girls at Malalai, she wanted desperately *not* to have a tragic ending. Perhaps it was time for women to be living heroines, not just martyrs.

When Meena was fifteen, in the tenth grade, she enrolled in Madame Sadaf's math and science class. These were not Meena's strongest subjects, but she tried hard because she liked the teacher very much. Madame Sadaf was tall and strode rapidly through the halls on long slim legs. She commanded respect from the girls with her husky-sounding voice. She was only twenty-five years old, not much older than her students, and she liked making friends with them. Her name, Sadaf, means "pearl," and to Meena, she was like a jewel of a teacher.

"You girls should appreciate your time at Malalai," Sadaf told them, "because many others do not have a chance to come here." One day when a group of girls were gathered around Sadaf after school, sitting on the grass under one of the trees, she confided her own story: "No one helped me to go to school. Back in 1959, when I was only thirteen, I came here on my own, holding hands with my neighbor, another girl who was a student here," Sadaf told them. "I just walked in through the gate one morning and asked to be allowed to learn."

Sadaf explained that her mother died when she was very young. She said, "When I reached the end of sixth grade, my father told me I had learned enough. He said I could read the Koran and that was all a girl needed. He said he needed me to work at home. So on my own, I went to the teachers at Malalai for help. I had no notebook. My stockings were torn, and my one pair of old shoes had been mended with nails that stuck out. The teachers let me stay for a few days to prove to them that I knew how to behave myself and study.

"I did well, but the principal told me that someone from my family must come and enroll me. So I convinced my aunt to come to school with me and give permission.

"Every day at school I felt sad, seeing how other children had parents to love them, while I was on my own, with no one to encourage me. I cannot say that I am like the real Malalai, but I was inspired by her example. I did all the housework at home, took care of the younger children, and worked very hard in school until I graduated. I went on to Teacher's College, and majored in math and science. When I finished, I was asked to join the faculty at Lycée Malalai."

Madame Sadaf was a role model for Meena. Her story convinced Meena that education was the answer for poor women, and made her more determined than ever to become someone who could help others.

Not all of Malalai's teachers were kind and encouraging to the girls. Some were strict and stern. One day, Meena was walking with a friend who was very shy. In an effort to look prettier, the friend had worn lipstick to school, which was forbidden. A teacher the girls always tried to avoid accosted the girl. "What's this on your face?" she demanded. She took out her handkerchief and roughly scrubbed the girl's face. "If you come here with this again, don't bother to come back at all."

The girl was paralyzed with fear, and her eyes filled with tears. To the teacher's amazement, Meena spoke up. "Please do not be so mean to her," Meena said, politely but firmly.

The teacher got even angrier and demanded, "Are you her defense attorney?"

Meena answered her calmly: "I'm not her defense attorney. But she's shy, and so I'm speaking for her."

The teacher was flustered and simply commanded them both: "Get into your class this minute!"

Madame Sadaf was standing in the doorway of her classroom and witnessed this exchange. She knew what it was like to need a defender at school, and her heart went out to Meena. Later, when she asked Meena about the incident, Meena said, "It was incredible, actually, because I do want to be a defense attorney, and maybe even a judge, so that I can defend women in the courts."

3

STUDY THE
KORAN WELL

Malalai was not a religious school. There were no daily prayers, although all of the Muslim girls took a class in reading the Koran, the Holy Book of Islam. The Hindu girls were excused from Koran class, and no one stigmatized them for their faith. Afghan tradition, with its roots in the most tolerant teachings of Islam, taught respect for different cultures and beliefs. The Sufi sect of Islam, which promoted fraternity with other religious groups was strong in Afghanistan.

Above all, Islam asks of its followers that they act with kindness and charity toward others. These traditional values had helped Afghans with different tribal, ethnic, religious, and linguistic backgrounds live together in relative peace. Afghans love life, and Islam allowed them to celebrate it with music, dance, and poetry.

The most famous Afghan poet was the Sufi Jelaluddin Balkhi, who is known in the West as Rumi. His life and poems were taught at Malalai. Rumi was born in 1207 in Balkh, Afghanistan, and later lived and wrote in what is now Turkey. Rumi's poems are ecstatic, mystical, mixed with folklore and jokes, and many believe they speak the happy wisdom of Islam.

At Malalai, Islamic culture meant that the girls were required to be modest, respectful to their teachers, and helpful to each other.

In the eighth grade, students could choose to study Arabic as well as French. If they learned Arabic, they would be able to read

Meena wearing her
Malalai High
School uniform.

the Koran in its original language. There was a class for older students on the interpretation of the Koran, but it was not required. Meena chose to take the advanced Koran class, because of her interest in law.

Under the "Royal Democracy" of the king, Afghanistan was governed by a constitution, not by the Koran. But the Afghan court system followed laws derived from interpretations of the Koran. The college of law at Kabul University where Meena hoped to study, was called the College of Sharia—the word for the law in the Koran. The Sharia is, literally, the path to the water, or the straight road of Islamic law.

The first thing Meena's teachers emphasized was that there were nearly a billion Muslims in the world, living in dozens of nations, and that the complex faith of Islam cannot be simplified. Interpretation of the Koran is very complex, and everything from human rights to criminal law in Muslim nations depends upon it. The Sharia law originated in a time when Muslim peoples were farmers or nomads, and its adjustment to modern technological and urban life has been difficult.

There was and is tremendous tension within Islam about how to interpret the six thousand verses of the Koran, many of which offer contradictory teachings. Meena and her friends were especially interested in the verse about the veiling of women. They discussed it endlessly.

"The veil has been controversial from the beginning," one of the girls said. Everyone knew that the Prophet Mohammed's first wife, Khadija, was a powerful and wealthy businesswoman who supported him financially. "Khadija never veiled or secluded herself," Meena pointed out. "She never even stopped working at her trading business."

It was during Mohammed's long marriage to Khadija that he began to hear the voice that he and his followers believed conveyed the word of Allah. The Koran is the record of the verses revealed to Mohammed.

After Khadija's death, Mohammed married again and again, until he had as many as nine wives at one time. The most controversial of his brides was Aisha, the former wife of his own adopted son. It was on his wedding night to her that Mohammed voiced the instruction for his followers on how they should approach his wives.

Meena said, "Madame Nooria says that the only verse about women's clothing is the one that says, 'If you ask Mohammed's wives for anything, speak to them from behind a curtain. This is purer for your hearts and their hearts.'"

From this verse comes the rule that pious Muslim women should cover their bodies with veils. The word for the veil is *hijab*, which literally means "curtain" in Arabic. To Meena and her friends, the verse did not require women to be covered.

"If a woman wants to wear it, she should," Meena said. "But I for one will never marry a man who wants me to."

Another girl agreed. "I don't want to parade around in a bikini, but I don't want to hide myself under a stupid cloth either."

In Afghanistan, the *hijab* was hotly contested. King Zahir Shah tried to abolish it. He ordered that the wives and daughters of Afghan diplomats not wear the veil. In 1959, at a ceremony marking the fortieth anniversary of Afghanistan's 1919 victory over the British, high-ranking members of the cabinet, military, and the royal family appeared on a viewing stand with their wives, all of them dressed in Western dress, with bare heads.

Some conservative Mullahs dared to protest against the king. They fomented riots, which were quelled by the police. The king had the rebellious Mullahs jailed, and then sent a senior scholar of the Koran to challenge them to show him where in the Holy Book they could point to any verse that requires women to be veiled. Only after they conceded that they could find no such verse were they freed.

Hijab takes such varied forms in Muslim countries that it ranges from a small, colorful head scarf in North Africa, where women also wear body-hugging dresses and open-toed sandals with nail polish, to a full-body black *abayah* in Saudi Arabia that covers everything, even cloaking a woman's eyes behind a black mesh. But the interpretation of the *Sharia*—the Islamic law—puts at stake far more serious matters of law for women than how they dress.

Women in some Muslim countries live their entire lives secluded in their homes. They may visit close relatives, but they do not venture out in public, even to go to a mosque to pray. They never work outside their homes, and in some places are forbidden by law to drive cars.

Sharia has been turned into a legal code that in many nations can deny a woman the right to inherit property. In some countries she must obtain permission from her father, husband, or brother before she can work, obtain a passport, or travel. In some nations, a woman's testimony is worthless in court. In its most extreme form, *Sharia* courts may sentence a married woman to death by stoning for the crime of adultery, even if the sexual contact was rape.

In Afghanistan, under the law, women were regarded as "half of men." The testimony of two women in court equaled the word of one man. If a man killed or injured another man, the murderer's family would have to give two girls in marriage to the victim's family, to settle the dispute.

Sharia law forced a wife to agree if her husband wished to take three more wives, but gave him the right to divorce her at his whim, while giving him absolute custody of her children. But a woman had no right to divorce a husband.

For Meena, the most painful part of the *Sharia* code was its tolerance of violence against women. *Sharia* allowed a husband to beat his wife if she disobeys. In her own life, there was something Meena never talked about to her friends or teachers. Though her family life at home was generally harmonious, sometimes there were fights. When her mother and stepmother argued, Meena's father became very angry. His word was the law in the house. Latif expected his wives to obey him without question or argument. If they were not instantly silent, he would lose his temper and strike them both. This was not unusual, even in middle-class homes like Meena's. Her grandfather had also struck her grandmother, she knew.

Meena loved her father, but she dared not speak up against his authority. Her heart wept for her mother and stepmother and burned with anger against her father when he lost his temper and lashed out. The fact that there were two wives did not increase their power. Both of them knew that they could be divorced at Latif's whim. The law gave Latif the power and perfect right to reject both his wives in favor of a third, younger wife. When her father hit her mothers, the utter powerlessness of every Afghan woman was brought home to Meena.

Meena promised herself never to agree to a marriage in which she would be confined and treated as her husband's servant. She dreamed of the new kind of marriage all of her girlfriends wanted: a marriage based on love and respect, a partnership of equals. Their role models were their married teachers. Many of them had children, yet still taught school.

"I'm going to marry only for love," Meena told her best friends. "I want a life like Madame Nooria has. Her husband encourages her career."

In Meena's advanced Koran class, the teachers taught liberal interpretations that supported women's right to happiness in marriage. For example, Malalai's students were taught that the verses that allow men to take more than one wife originated in a time of war when there were many widows among Mohammed's followers. He meant for men to take widows as wives so that they would not be destitute. It has become a frequent practice, however, for men to take young, unwed girls as their second, third, and fourth wives. Meena's teachers spoke against this custom, which grew up centuries after the death of Mohammed. They also told the girls about women in various Muslim nations who were working as politicians, teaching at universities, and serving in military forces.

It was not easy for the girls to understand exactly what the Koran mandated. Only about six hundred of its verses—just one-tenth of the total—concern family law, contracts, and criminal law.

They also needed to study the *hadith*, an additional body of teachings about the life of the Prophet Mohammed. For two centuries after his death, the *hadith* was compiled by people who had known Mohammed or who remembered stories about what he said and did. These stories preserve every detail of his behavior. Some actions or sayings attributed to the prophet have acquired the force of law.

A third source of *Sharia* law is not found in either the Koran or the *hadith*. Mohammed is believed to have said, "My community will not agree upon an error." This statement leaves open the question of what the Prophet meant by an error, and allows room for Mullahs to create many additional laws not found in the Koran at all.

The complications of the law fascinated Meena. Madame Nooria had taught her: "Afghan women have always been oppressed, abused, and degraded by their families, their fathers, and their husbands. Most do not know what their rights are. They do not even know they have rights." Madame Nooria openly taught the girls the idea of secularism—the separation of government from religion. She believed that religious practice should be up to the individual, and that government should apply the laws equally to everyone, regardless of belief or gender.

What Meena wanted more than anything was to study *Sharia* and become an attorney. If she could one day become a judge, she could make the greatest difference for women. Meena felt desperately that she wanted to help women win their most basic freedoms. She devoured books that told the life stories of women who resisted tyranny.

Madame Nooria gave Meena a biography of Jamila Bopasha, an Algerian woman who had fought against the French. Malalai School was founded by the French, and Meena admired France and its culture. But no one could deny that the French had colonized Algeria, a Muslim nation in North Africa, from 1830 until the war of resistance finally won the country's independence in 1962. Jamila Bopasha was born in 1938 during the colonial regime. She was taken prisoner at the age of twenty-three when French soldiers raided her family's home. They turned the house upside down and beat Jamila, her elderly father, and even her pregnant sister. Jamila refused to tell them anything, so they took her to prison and tortured her with electric shocks. She still refused to talk.

Eventually, two Frenchwomen, both of them attorneys, found out about Jamila and publicized her case. Jamila became a *cause célèbre* in France, and the story of her suffering was one of the reasons the French public ultimately turned against the war in Algeria. People were shocked to realize the double standards applied to their own citizens and the people in the colony. Eventually, Jamila was freed and lived to see Algeria's independence.

For Meena, the story of Jamila's resistance was inspiring. But even more important to Meena was the example of the role played by the brave women who were Jamila's lawyers. Meena was sure she could argue for justice also.

What Meena was learning in school reinforced the ideals her parents had taught her at home. Islam teaches that the even the weakest and most vulnerable person should be treated with charity and respect. To Afghans, *hamsai-ag*—neighborliness—is one of the most important values. The ideal is that everyone has the duty to care for each other, especially in times of crisis, regardless of religion or ethnicity. But not everyone in any culture lives up to its ideals.

Meena took seriously what adults taught her. But she could not blind herself to the fact that much of what she had been taught contrasted sharply with the reality she saw around her. She could not stand the hypocrisy of people who professed to be devout Muslims, and respectable citizens, yet mistreated people they considered to be beneath them.

Meena witnessed injustice next door to her own home. Her reading was often interrupted by the disturbing sound of angry voices carrying over the courtyard wall. She could hear the neighbors harshly giving orders to Shama, the servant girl they kept. Meena could not bear to hear the girl being abused. She felt like calling out, "Leave her alone!" But she knew better than to interfere.

Shama got up before dawn to bake bread and begin cooking for the large family she served. Then she cleaned the floors, served the meals, and washed the dishes and pots. She did the laundry until late at night. Shama was an Hazara, like many servants in Kabul.

The Hazaras are a minority people from the central part of Afghanistan. They are said to be descended from the thousand soldiers the Mongolian invader Genghis Khan left behind when he swept through Afghanistan in the thirteenth century. The word *Hazara* means "thousand" in Farsi. The Hazaras have Asian features, which make them easy to identify and discriminate against. Many were enslaved when they were conquered by the Pashtuns in the late nineteenth century. Hazara girls were treated like property. They could be given as servants to pay debts, or to settle disputes.

Until the king outlawed the practice in the 1920s, wealthy men kept Hazara women as slave concubines.

Meena was a Pashtun, but she felt a special responsibility to side with people who suffered from Pashtun domination and prejudice. Meena's mother told a family friend, "My daughter Meena is different from my other children. You can't compare her to anyone else in the family. She studies all the time, and she is always worrying, especially about poor people."

Meena always greeted Shama politely when she saw her in the street, even though most people thought Hazaras should be ignored. Plenty of other people in the neighborhood treated Shama like a dirty creature far beneath them. Even little children ordered her around or hit her.

Meena's joy in a new pair of fashionable shoes drained away when she had to walk past Shama, who was so poor that she wore a pair of cast-off soldiers' combat boots too big for her. Meena had trouble swallowing bites from the big platters of meat and rice served at home when she knew Shama was eating only a scrap of bread with boiled greens.

Lying awake in her bed at night, Meena heard Shama crying. Her husband, who was also a poor Hazara laborer, was beating her again. He came home exhausted, but many nights he was not too tired to beat Shama. The whole time he was hitting her, he berated her cruelly, because she had borne him no children. Meena pulled a pillow over her head to try to block out his angry shouts and Shama's pitiful cries. She wept along with Shama, reminded of the times when her own mothers had to bow down under her father's blows.

Meena could hardly stand looking at Shama's bruised and swollen face when the servant girl went to the neighborhood market. Meena was kind to her, and asked her questions about her life. She found out that Shama's parents were so poor that they had sold her into marriage to her much older husband when she was eleven. Even the tiny bride-price for such a girl could stave off a family's starvation in a time of drought and famine.

Meena was just a teenaged girl. There was nothing she could do. The law said that it was a man's right to beat his wife, and no one would stop it. Even when a marriage was as miserably unhappy as Shama's, divorce was still not possible. If Shama had tried to run away, she could have been locked up in Kabul's horrifying women's prison. Her husband could even have killed her for running away, and he would not have been punished.

Meena seethed with frustration, and tried to concentrate on women she had read about who would never have tolerated anyone beating them. She thought about Jack London's wife, Charmian, who sailed around the world as Jack's equal and partner.

Meena knew that until the law was changed, no woman would have the right to leave a man who beat her, let alone have him arrested and charged with assault. All Meena could do was to work hard at school, go to the university, and become a lawyer. It was for poor women that Meena wanted to study law. She wanted to learn how to defend the Shamas of Afghanistan.

Meena idolized Joan of Arc, the symbol of female rebellion and the perfect heroine for an Afghan girl to love. So much of Afghanistan seemed to exist in the fourteenth century, it was easy to picture Joan riding out on horseback to face her enemies with a sword in her hand. The girls at Malalai were assigned to read *The Lark*, a French play that brought to life the sixteen-year-old future saint who had dressed as a man to lead an army of men against the English.

Joan's words, preserved in the actual transcript of her 1430 trial, sounded contemporary in Afghanistan: "I am an illiterate peasant girl, the same as any other in my village."

The Inquisitor asks Joan, "Don't you think you would have done better to sew and spin beside your mother?"

She replies: "I had something else to do, my lord. There have always been plenty of women to do women's work."

Confronting seventy stern male judges, Joan declared, "Don't think I haven't been afraid. I was afraid all the time, from the very beginning, which is nobody's business but mine . . . You get through because you think deeper, imagine more, and get over your fear first."

Meena's classmates imagined that Joan's inquisitors were like the Mullahs who had the power to impose harsh sentences on women. When the judges threatened Joan with burning at the stake, she told them, "You have a right to hit me with all your power. And my right is to say NO, and go on believing."

Meena could almost imagine herself at the head of a ragged army of servant girls like Shama.

4

THE NEW WORLD BEGINS

On July 17, 1972, a momentous event took place. The king was overthrown! The news reached Malalai School within hours. The students poured into the schoolyard during their break and stood talking in tense, excited groups.

"My mother graduated from Malalai in the same class with one of the royal princesses," one girl said. "What is going to happen to them?"

It was frightening to imagine the country without the king. For generations, Afghans had been taught that their duty was to obey first Allah and then the king. King Zahir's ancestors, the Durrani family, had ruled Afghanistan for 250 years.

"My parents said the monarchy could not last forever," another girl said. "But who is going to replace the king? He is the only leader we know."

"There is nothing to take his place," a worried teacher said.

There had been no fighting. While King Zahir was traveling in Europe, his cousin, Prince Sardar Daoud, had taken power and declared Afghanistan a republic, and, without an election, he declared himself president.

Meena and the other girls knew of Prince Daoud from their history class. He was Afghanistan's former prime minister. In the early 1960s, Prince Daoud had wanted to build up an army to defend Afghanistan, and he had asked the United States for military aid. The Cold War was at its height, and the U. S. and the Soviet Union were competing for supremacy in every part of the world. They vied for decades to gain influence over Afghanistan, but when Prince Daoud asked, the U.S. refused to give the aid. Daoud then turned to the Soviet Union, which welcomed the opportunity to extend its influence over its neighbor to the south. The U.S.S.R. poured arms and money into Afghanistan. Prince Daoud had been responsible for many reforms, but for the pro-Western king, this was going too far. The king fired Daoud in 1963. Now, nine years later, Prince Daoud had overthrown the king.

It was impossible for the girls at Malalai to study as usual. The teachers herded them into class, but no one could concentrate. What did anyone care about math or French when everything was falling apart around them? Debates were taking place in every high school courtyard all over the city. No one knew what was going to happen.

Madame Nooria decided to turn her class over to the girls' questions. Many students, like Meena, were children of parents close to the king's government. "What will happen to our parents' jobs?" they asked her. "Will everyone who was working for the king be fired?" Madame Nooria did her best to calm the girls. Rumors flew, and quickly the truth emerged: During the years he was out of office, Prince Daoud had made an alliance with the small, secretive, pro-Soviet Afghan Communist Party, *Parcham*—the Flag. Many *Parcham* members had been educated in the Soviet Union and were pro-Soviet. *Parcham* was mostly centered in the cities, especially among university students and army officers. Their leader was a man named Babrak Karmal. It was these men who had helped Daoud to take over the government.

Though she tried to reassure her students, Madame Nooria's grim face revealed her own apprehension. She talked frankly to the girls about the Soviet Union's terrible record to the north of Afghanistan: They had suppressed the people's Muslim religion, had wreaked vast environmental damage, forced the people to move onto government-run collective farms, and denied them freedom of speech.

"If this is what *Daoud* and Parcham want to bring to Afghanistan," she told the class, "we must be prepared to oppose them with all our strength,"

Daoud immediately formed a pro-Soviet government modeled on the autocratic Communist Party of the Soviet Union. He moved at once to arrest or drive out members of the king's government and anyone else who did not support their coup. Many people loyal to the king were imprisoned, or left the country to join the king in exile.

At home, Meena's family faced a crossroads. Her father Latif was in danger of being fired, or even arrested. Latif had to decide what to do. Some people who tried to declare loyalty to the new regime were fired anyway. Meena's uncles and male cousins gathered to discuss the situation. Fortunately, Latif's job as an architect was not a political one, and he was close to retirement age. He decided to quit his government work to avoid being fired or arrested. Meena's older brothers went to work to contribute to the family's income.

Prince Daoud and his *Parcham* allies opened the country to Soviet influence. Russian doctors, teachers, engineers, and technicians flooded into Afghanistan. They provided many useful aid projects, but everything they offered came with heavy strings attached. In the countryside, the Soviets had grandiose plans for enormous dams, huge irrigation projects, and highways that displaced people and animals. In agrarian Afghanistan, the Soviet technocratic society clashed with one of the last strongholds of feudalism. The Soviets gave Prince Daoud's regime money and military aid that strengthened its undemocratic rule. The United States, distracted by its war in Vietnam, had little official presence in Kabul. America did not see Afghanistan as a foreign-policy priority.

Still, American influence in Kabul was already strong in the form of Western youth culture. European and American tourists, many of them young hippies, roamed Afghanistan in their jeans and miniskirts, hitchhiking, sleeping outside along the roads, eating together in restaurants, some smoking marijuana and opium. Older Afghans treated them with customary hospitality and courtesy, but kept their distance from them. Young people, however, were attracted to their music and carefree ways. A movie theater, the Zainab Cinema, opened in Kabul, where young blue-jeans-wearing Afghans flocked to see Russian, European, and Indian movies.

There was another source of change brewing in Kabul. Many Afghans were struggling to meld the old with the new, but at the university, one professor preached a fanatical new doctrine in reaction to the new ways. His name was Berhanuddin Rabbani, and he taught in the Sharia Law College. He and a band of students close to him felt so threatened by the modern ways that were rushing into Afghanistan from all sides, that they formulated an outright rejection of all things modern and foreign. They based their rejection on religion and preached a new form of Islam they called "pure."

Rabbani and his followers sought refuge in new, extremely narrow interpretations of the Prophet Mohammed's life. They defended their ideas with justifications long since discredited in the West, such as the idea that pregnancy and menstruation make it impossible for women to work outside their homes.

To these men, fanaticism was a simple way to bring order to a life that felt chaotic. They declared war on the rest of Muslims, especially Muslim women, and on all non-Muslims. They were fundamentalists; that is, they wanted to return to the teachings they considered to be the fundamental, literal words of God as told to the Prophet. They thought that if only everyone would willingly go back to the old ways, society would be repaired and peace would return. But many people were not willing to follow them, and those people they attacked.

Rabbani and his followers took it upon themselves to demand that women students leave the university altogether. But far from leaving, women walked happily arm in arm everywhere across the campus. They were taking up new areas of study, including engineering and architecture. Many were wearing Western dress, even the short skirts that were fashionable in the West at the time. In Professor Rabbani's conservative view, female students were an insult to Islamic custom. He preached that the West was rotten with moral decay, and the answer was a return to ancient ways and strict adherence to a rigid code of behavior.

One of the most rabid among Rabbani's followers was Gulbaddin Hekmatyar, one of the founders of a political party called *Hezb-e-Islami*—the Islamic Party.

Rabbani incited his small group of male followers to action. They attacked women on the campus, throwing caustic acid onto their bare legs and leaving painful burns. The angry men even tried to splash the acid into the women's faces. The injuries were serious.

As the attackers threw the acid they yelled at the women, "Cover your faces and legs!" "Go home where you belong!" and, "The university is not for women!" They called the women "whores" and "un-Islamic."

No one arrested the fundamentalists—apparently the police looked the other way.

The disturbing news of the attacks on women students reached the courtyard of Malalai High School, carried by the older brothers and sisters of Meena's friends, who were studying at the university.

In only another year or two, Meena and her classmates hoped to enroll at the university themselves. The girls at Malalai could talk of nothing but the acid attacks. What was the point of studying so hard if they were not going to be welcomed at the university when they graduated? How could these men get away with injuring women? Meena and her friends were horrified and frightened.

In response, the principals of many schools in the city allowed thousands of their female students to leave school to demonstrate against the attacks. They marched to the university and held a rally demanding the arrest of the attackers. There were speeches in favor of democracy and women's education. But in spite of the demonstration, the government did not act against the fanatics.

A 1972 demonstration by Kabul High School girls. Their signs call for democracy. Courtesy of Laurence Brun/Rapho.

Madame Sadaf, Meena's science and math teacher, took time from a physics lesson to talk about the attacks. "This discussion," she told them, "is not far off the topic of science, because it is about the role of science in relation to the role of religion.

"Nothing the prophet ever spoke could lead to burning girls with acid," she began. "The Koran says, 'Treat your women well, and be kind to them.' To attack women also violates our Afghan culture, which teaches *nang*—honor. Nang is about the duty to respect and protect women. What these foolish young men have done violates Islamic law and the message of Islam. They want to drag Afghanistan back to a time even before Islam."

She listed on the chalkboard the elements of the extremists' doctrine: antiwoman, anti-intellectual, antiprogress, antiscience.

"These beliefs are destructive to Islam," she said, "because they distort Islam's tradition of learning. The oldest universities in the world are Islamic—much older than many in the West. Muslim women can be scholars, too.

"These men do not know that Mohammed was among the world's greatest reformers on behalf of women. Before the Prophet, ignorant people buried girl babies alive. Mohammed outlawed female infanticide. He abolished slavery also. Widows used to be forced to marry their husbands' brothers, whether they wanted to or not. Mohammed freed them from that. He guaranteed women the right to inherit property and the right to control their own wealth.

"According to our religion, women have a perfect right to take part in society. You girls can faithfully practice Islam and at the same time you can become engineers and doctors. You have a duty to learn all you can about science and health and bring these to our people. If we don't take the lead to bring Afghanistan into the modern world, non-Afghans and non-Muslims will do it."

One of the girls raised her hand. "If what they say is not Islam, why do they say it is?"

Madame Sadaf answered, "They want religious people to believe them. They say they want to go back to the fundamentals of religion. But it's not true that they are following Muslim traditions. Fundamentalism is growing in Christianity, Judaism, and Hinduism also. In all cases, it's a movement that appeals to people who are afraid of change. I think there's a lot to criticize about modern life, but the answer is to take the new ways and use them for good. The answer is not to turn to violence."

Another girl asked: "If the extremists hate the modern world, why do they go to the university? Why do they drive in cars and print leaflets about their beliefs? Why don't they go to the mountains where they could live like in ancient times?"

"What do you girls think?" Madame Sadaf asked.

"I think they stay in the city because they want to get power over everyone else," one student answered.

"Do you think they'll be able to take power?" Meena asked.

"No, they will never win," Madame Sadaf replied. "But you girls are right. They want to impose their views on other people, and I think they are dangerous. All of us will have to work hard against them. Study the Koran well, so that you will know what the prophet really told us."

Another girl had a question, "If they are against science," she asked, "why don't they attack the science and engineering labs at the university or the foreign professors who are teaching?"

"I think it's because they are afraid to attack anyone powerful," Madame Sadaf answered. "It's easier for them to throw acid on innocent girls."

Madame Sadaf tried to encourage her students to be brave. "You mustn't let these extremists discourage you from studying. It's your right to go to the university. These men are the most ignorant people there. No one worthy of your respect respects them. Gulbaddin Hekmatyar may win over a few confused people. There will always be some who are looking for answers in a list of rules instead of in the scientific inquiry I am teaching to you. But someone like Gulbaddin will never be able to take over. Now open your books."

Meena trusted her teachers, but still, the violence of the fanatics frightened her. Professor Rabbani's band was centered in the *Sharia* College, where she hoped to enroll. There were some professors there who were more tolerant, but still, studying law would be an act of tremendous courage. Meena wished she could be welcomed by all of the students and professors, but she knew that some would reject her just for being a woman.

Madame Nooria reassured her that there were many democratic organizations and many teachers and students at the university who thought as she did. "Education is the only long-term solution to prevent young people from being attracted to extreme fundamentalism," Madame Nooria told Meena. "Your job is to go and study and teach others."

Meena looked forward to attending the university and joining with other students. She especially respected one outspoken university student named Saidal Sukhandan. He was well-known as a talented firebrand of a poet who wrote about the lives of the peasants, and also known for his moving speeches against both the pro-Soviets of the Daoud and *Parcham* regime and the Islamic fundamentalists. Sukhandan was twenty-four while she was sixteen. He was someone Meena admired from afar, and she hoped someday to hear him give a speech.

In spite of the opposition to the Islamic fundamentalists on campus, they continued to grow in number, and they fought among themselves for power. Not only were they intolerant of women, but they hated people of other ethnic groups. Unable to tolerate each other, they soon split along ethnic lines. Soon, the Tajik leaders Rabbani and Masood split off and formed their own party, leaving Hekmatyar and Sayyaf, both Pashtuns, to run the Islamic Party— *Hezb-e-Islami*. They split into smaller and smaller factions as they argued over their more and more narrow interpretations of the Koran and the *hadith*. Both factions escalated their violence on campus.

The next year, the fundamentalists decided to come, uninvited, to a prodemocracy rally that was called at the university. They came armed. As Saidal Sukhandan spoke, reading his poems to the crowd, shots rang out. The young poet was killed. Witnesses said that Gulbaddin Hekmatyar was the one who had fired the shots. In spite of protests by Sukhandan's supporters, no one was arrested.

For Meena, the news of Sukhandan's death came as a wounding blow. Her beliefs and feelings were so close to his that she could not stop thinking, "It could have been me." She was a senior, soon to graduate, but the hope of learning in a peaceful atmosphere evaporated with the smoke from Gulbaddin Hekmatyar's pistol.

Then the extremist bands made a mistake. They tried to attack Prince Daoud's government, and Daoud cracked down on them. Some were arrested. Most of them, though—including Gulbaddin Hekmatyar—escaped over the Pakistan border to the frontier city of Peshawar. There they set up several competing political parties, each one more extremist and violent than the last. The Pakistani regime, headed by an Islamist president, Zulfiqur Bhutto, gave them funds to help them survive. The Pakistani secret police—the Interservices Intelligence—began a close friendship with the fundamentalists that would last for decades.

Meena and her friends and teachers were relieved to see the Rabbani gang go. There were many moderate Mullahs and scholars at the university, and now the girls who had done well enough to be admitted could not wait to begin their studies.

Graduation was a proud day. Meena's hard work had earned her third place in her class. There was a reception, with refreshments. A representative from the Ministry of Education made a speech, as did Malalai's principal. The younger students wished the seniors a happy future. Meena's life in the wider world was about to begin.

5

A PARTNERSHIP

Kabul University in 1976 was like a boiling pot. In the soup were the ideas of Marx, Mao, and Mohammed. Western liberalism, Islamic teachings, and Afghan nationalism were all hotly debated.

The Daoud regime had been in power for three years, during which Afghanistan had become less and less stable. Seeking power for himself, Daoud had purged most of the *Parcham* members who had helped bring him to power. Daoud took billions in aid from the Soviets, but also turned to India, Saudi Arabia, and Iraq for help. Political student groups often clashed at the university over their opposing theories about Afghanistan's future. Besides the pro-Soviet *Parcham* and *Khalq* parties there were pro-China Maoist groups. Their ideas had little connection to Afghanistan's realities.

Meena read everything she could find. She listened and tried to make up her own mind. She already had her own strong ideas, influenced by both Western and Muslim ideas about freedom from oppression. Nationalism was natural to her because she loved her country and did not want to live under foreign domination. She wanted to choose among all of the ideas being debated, seeking a way that would be uniquely Afghan.

The *Sharia* College was especially filled with turmoil. Every issue was debated there, and Meena found herself in the midst of heated discussions over questions of women's roles. Women were free to raise their hands and speak in class, and Meena was among the most outspoken.

Though the university was coeducational, women did not socialize with men. Meena and her women friends walked to and from the campus together. In class, they sat together.

Meena was unusual because she did not mind calling attention to herself. One of Meena's male cousins was also a student at the university. She liked him, but he was old-fashioned. One day, she made him his favorite dish—yogurt and cucumbers—and brought it to campus for him. As a joke, she boldly called him out of class and handed it to him in front of his friends. Meena knew her conservative cousin was caught between family loyalty and embarrassment, and she gave him a big mischevious grin. He had to laugh.

At political rallies, Meena stood with her women friends at the edge of the crowd. Very few women stood up to give speeches, but they listened and discussed what they were hearing.

The student debates were not an empty exercise in philosophy. Student movements all over the world had changed the direction of whole nations. Young people were changing governments, leading cultural revolutions, stopping wars or starting them. Many students were convinced that in a very short time the world would be different, and that they would be the ones to transform it.

The political organizations on campus did not appeal to Meena. Most did not even allow women to join, and to Meena, those that did were not worth joining, because the women had such subservient roles. To Meena, the most important issue was women's rights. No matter what idea someone suggested, she looked at its effect on the lives of women. Also, it was impossible for Meena to think about "women's issues" without thinking about society as a whole. She knew poor and uneducated women could never be free. To change those realities, she thought, society would have to be changed. Freedom for women, in Meena's mind, was more revolutionary than anything she heard in all the speeches the men were making. True women's equality would change everything from the inside out.

Europe had a stronger influence on Meena and other young Afghans than Latin America, China, or the Muslim nations. The ideas of European and American professors at the university played an important role in the debates. Meena was most attracted to the constitutions of France, England, and the Scandinavian nations. She worked hard to study various judicial systems, looking for rights granted to women. She knew there was no nation where women's lives were perfect, but in some, they enjoyed real protections under the laws. Meena recognized that medical care, education, and freedom of religion were crucial to women's advancement.

Meena was also looking for a way out of her own dilemma. How could she possibly pursue her studies, build a career, and help other women, yet at the same time fall in love, marry, and have children? Her beauty and intelligence attracted the notice of many male students, but nice Afghan girls did not meet men unless they were introduced through their families. They did not date. Men had to approach Meena through her relatives with an offer of marriage, and some did so. She rejected every one of them, because they did not even try to hide the fact that as soon as she married them, she would have to leave her studies. Some even offered money to her parents—the traditional dowry or bride-price that Meena thought was barbaric.

More and more of Meena's friends from high school were leaving their studies and disappearing behind walls. Meena dreaded sharing their fate. She knew she not only had to avoid an old-fashioned, restrictive husband, but she had to watch out for controlling and demanding in-laws. As a traditional wife, a woman was expected to move into her husband's family home and help with the housework there. Traditionally, the most powerful time in a woman's life came when she could dominate the lives of her son's wives. If Meena made the wrong marriage, she might exchange her supportive parents for backward parents-in-law.

Like other girls, Meena had a host of relatives who had been thinking about a match for her since the year she was born. Her aunt, especially, thought it was her duty to find Meena a husband. She reminded Meena every time she saw her of the old saying, "A girl is a guest in the house of her parents."

"But, Aunt, *jan*—Aunt dear," Meena said, "I'm having a wonderful time at the university. I don't want to give up my books for wedding plans. And you know I'll never marry any man who will confine me to the house."

"Meena, you are nineteen," her aunt protested, "much older than the age when most girls marry. You cannot simply remain single. You are too vulnerable to the advances of men. You should choose someone while you have a chance. Otherwise, in the end, your father will choose for you."

"Even if I choose a man, how do I know he won't take another wife later on? I will not agree to marry anyone who won't promise me he will never do that. Also, anyone I marry must let me go on with my studies."

The most desirable marriage was between first cousins, whose ties to the extended family would be strengthened by a match within it. But Meena would not have any of her cousins. Even though she loved them, they were all too conservative for her.

The pressure to marry was increasing every day Meena went to the university without a wedding ring on her finger. As a single girl she was pursued constantly, and she began to think that if she were married to the right kind of man, she would actually be able to study and work with more freedom.

But in the Kabul of 1976, the right kind of man was hard to find. As Meena firmly told her inquiring aunt, she had set conditions: She must be allowed to continue her studies, to work as an attorney, and she must be the only wife.

One day, Meena's aunt told Meena's mother, "I have an idea. My cousin knows a handsome, eligible medical doctor who has never been married. He is Dr. Faiz Ahmed, and he is distantly related to our family."

Meena's aunt's cousin told Meena's parents that she had checked on Dr. Ahmed's reputation and heard good things about him. His father had died when he was young. He was the oldest of several children, and he had been devoted to his mother. As soon as he was old enough, he had supported her and helped her raise his younger siblings. Later, he had cared for his mother until her recent death.

"No parents-in-law," Meena's aunt commented. "It is sad not to have their love and support, but maybe for our headstrong Meena, it would be an advantage."

Dr. Ahmed practiced medicine, but he was also a political activist, interested in many of the same issues that concerned Meena. "He sounds very suitable," Meena's aunt said. "Now if Meena will only agree to consider him."

The cousin made all the contacts. When Dr. Faiz had heard all about Meena, he asked her parents for her hand. They considered his qualifications, which seemed excellent. It occurred to them also, that with Meena's delicate health, her seizures and painful legs, marriage to a doctor would be another advantage. Meena's parents gave their approval.

Meena was not so sure, but she agreed at least to meet Faiz. In traditional times, Afghan couples did not even see each other until their wedding day. In the old-fashioned ceremony, a mirror was placed on the floor in front of the kneeling couple. When they looked into it, they saw each other's faces for the first time.

Contrary to that tradition, Meena insisted on talking to Faiz, to see for herself if she and he could make a life together.

Faiz Ahmed came to her home for their first meeting. When the nineteen-year-old Meena walked into the room with her mother and first saw him, he seemed to her like a man of another generation. He was eleven years older: thirty. But his face was so friendly, with deep lines alongside his full mouth that came from smiling and laughing, that she couldn't help smiling, too. He was so much a Pashtun that he could have been her close relative. He had her same dark hair, prominent eyebrows and nose, and expressive black eyes. She liked him, especially his sense of humor. He made her comfortable by making her laugh right away.

They talked about the first thing they had in common, Kabul University, where he had also studied. For Faiz, Meena was the kind of woman he had hardly dared to hope for—a wife he could talk to about the world around them. These were desperate times of exciting change. Meena wanted to be a part of it all just as much as Faiz did.

He explained to her that he was the leader of a socialist party. The Afghan Liberation Organization members were not Soviet-style communists. Like Meena, they were critical of the pro-Soviet Daoud government. His group looked to China, where a peasant army led by Mao Zedong had made a revolution, as a model for an agrarian-based society like Afghanistan. Faiz's group had members on campus, and Meena had heard of it. She was not sure she agreed with their ideas, but she definitely wanted to see the doctor again.

As they met and talked, Faiz assured Meena she did not have to agree with everything he thought. "I will always respect your right to hold your own opinions," he promised her.

It was hard for Meena at first to trust that he would keep his word to allow her to pursue her own goals. But as they grew closer, she could not help but believe he was sincere.

Faiz said he wanted Meena to finish her education and become an attorney or anything else she wanted to be. Like her, he did not believe in polygamy. He promised never even to consider taking another wife. To him, Meena was so lovely and intelligent, he could not imagine ever wanting anyone else.

Meena could hardly believe that such a man existed, someone who promised to support her ambitions and also to work alongside her for their country. He was the husband she had hardly dared to dream about, someone who shared her passion for ideas and commitment to the future of their nation. She didn't love Faiz, but in the end she decided she had found a kind, serious, and dedicated man, as much like her as any potential partner could be. She told him, and her parents, that she accepted his proposal.

Meena and Faiz talked for hours about books, history, and poetry. As they got to know one another, Meena told Faiz how the murder of the young socialist poet Saidal Sukhandan had affected her, how she reread his poems often and vowed always to remember him. When Faiz told her he had known Saidal well, and mourned him also, her heart opened toward him, and she began to fall in love.

Faiz wanted to introduce Meena to his friends, Shohib and Mowaish. Shohib was an older man, a military officer, and he and Faiz had been best friends for years. Shohib and his wife, Mowaish, had supported Faiz through the long hard time of his mother's last illness, and he visited them often. He took Meena with him to their home for tea.

As soon as Faiz and Meena arrived, Meena and Mowaish recognized each other and embraced. Mowaish and Shohib had several daughters younger than Meena who all studied at Malalai.

"I remember you from your graduation day!" Mowaish exclaimed. "My daughters always talked about how much they admired you when you were a senior, and they pointed you out to me."

Shohib and Mowaish were a modern couple who did not separate men from women for social occasions.

"Faiz is like my brother," Shohib said. "We are family." All four of them sat down together to share bowls of nuts and candies. Mowaish, pouring tea with a delighted smile, could not believe what good fortune this match was.

"Because Faiz is so nice, I always hoped he would marry someone wonderful," she whispered to Meena. "You wait to see who someone you love will marry, and you hope. Then you find out he loves someone you admire so much. It's just like a movie!"

Meena couldn't help laughing at Mowaish's enthusiasm, even though it was embarrassing to receive so much attention about her personal life from a stranger. She liked Mowaish and Shohib, and she was proud that Faiz had such good friends. Mowaish was quite a bit older than Meena. Her name means "stone," and Meena felt she was a solid person she could rely on.

When it came to planning a wedding, Faiz and Meena agreed that they would set a modern example. Traditional weddings were enormous, expensive affairs that lasted several days, even a week. Families went years into debt to pay for them. Hundreds of guests were fed, and the bride wore a different costly dress each day.

The payment of a *haq-o-mar*—a bride-price—was out of the question for them. Both Faiz and Meena hated the idea that a woman was bought from her father like a piece of property. Meena did not want anyone to go into debt or take money away from the younger children's educations to buy the gold bracelets Afghan brides were given when they left home.

Faiz and Meena also rejected the traditional custom of serving the wedding feast to men and women separately. Their simple celebration took place at Meena's parents' home. The men gathered in the main room, and the women in a smaller room. A Mullah, a local priest, first asked Faiz, in front of the male witnesses, whether he accepted Meena as his wife. Then he went into the other room where Meena, dressed in the traditional green dress symbolizing hope, waited with her sisters, friends, aunts, and mothers.

"Do you accept him as your husband?" he asked her.

"Yes," she said, excited, fearful and ready to cry from joy all at once.

The Mullah went back and forth between the two rooms, asking each of them the question three times. Then Meena and all of the women joined Faiz and the men. Faiz and Meena exchanged the simple silver bands they had chosen for their wedding rings.

When the religious ceremony was over, Meena changed into a white dress for the party. Platters were brought, heaped with rice, covered with pieces of roasted chicken and sprinkled with pomegranate seeds. Neighbors, friends, and relatives came to eat and wish the new couple a happy life.

Mowaish and Shohib were among the guests who came to offer their congratulations. Mowaish told them, "I admire you for your modern ways." On the way home she told her husband Shohib, "What great minds they have!"

Meena and Faiz moved into a modest house in the Karde Marmoeen—a working class neighborhood of Kabul. Right away, both of them resumed their busy lives. Faiz's medical practice occupied him, and the work of his political party consumed most of the rest of his time. Meena was just as busy with her studies, and running their household.

Most housewives spent hours on shopping, cooking, and cleaning. Meena squeezed all of this into her student life. As in many homes in Kabul, there was no running water in Faiz's and Meena's house. Every day Meena carried buckets to fetch water from the well of their friendly next-door neighbor.

From the beginning of their married life together, Faiz was preoccupied with the affairs of his small political party. In the early 1970s when Meena had still been a schoolgirl and Faiz was in his midtwenties, he had become a political leader, active in a large leftist movement known by the name of its journal, *Sholai Jowaid—The Eternal Flame*. In the late 1960s and early 1970s, the *Sholayis*, as they were called, were a much more popular movement in Kabul than either of the pro-Soviet *Khalq* or *Parcham* parties or the Islamic extremists. Thousands of Afghans rejected the influence of the United States, and were wary of the U.S.S.R. to the north. They were watching with interest the new society being born next door in China.

Mao's cultural revolution in China seemed to offer the poorest peasants a much better future, in just one generation. Chairman Mao sent millions of students—the Red Guards—to the countryside to teach villagers to read and write; land that had been owned by ruling families for centuries was confiscated and given to the landless; young "barefoot doctors" were trained to vaccinate children and provide hygiene and health care to people who had never before seen a physician.

The excesses of this campaign were hidden, and its advances were extolled all over the world. The Chinese government's propaganda campaigned to win people over, while suppressing dissenting intellectuals. There was no freedom of speech or press. The Chinese authorities were good at concealing the coercion behind their revolution. They smashed artworks, closed temples and monasteries, and hid the prisons, burned books, and performed executions that were the dark consequences for critics of the regime. Few even knew about China's suppression of Tibet.

Under the Daoud government in Afghanistan, Maoists like Faiz's *Sholayi* group were a beleaguered and harassed sect. Faiz frequently went to meetings of the *Sholayis*, and they often came to meetings at Meena and Faiz's house. They were frantically trying to educate people against the Daoud regime.

Meena found she was in agreement with some of the *Sholayis'* opinions. She shared their belief in the need for collective action. Both Meena and Faiz knew that little could be accomplished by individuals working alone.

Meena saw the need to take action, but she doubted that China's way was a blueprint for Afghanistan. She still held to her vision of a democratic, secular government that would guarantee civil rights. To her, a male-dominated Maoist party had little to offer ordinary Afghan women, and would have to change before it could involve many ordinary Afghans of either gender.

Meena and Faiz often visited Mowaish and Shohib, and all four of them had lively discussions.

Mowaish told Meena, "I'm amazed Faiz gives you the right to choose your own way. You're so independent of him. You even reject what he believes. It's very unusual."

Meena laughed. "This was our agreement from before we married."

As the Daoud regime grew more repressive, Meena agreed more and more with Faiz that opposition to it was a top priority. It was also desperately important to try to educate people about the danger the Soviets posed to Afghanistan. The results of Soviet rule were easy to see in the five central Asian republics to the north that had been swept into the Soviet empire. The independence of Kazakhstan, Kyrgyzstan, Tajikistan, Uzbekistan, and Turkmenistan was gone. They were captive Muslim lands ruled from Moscow by handpicked local managers. *Stan* is a Persian suffix that means "place"—thus, the place of the Afghans is Afghanistan. All of the *Stans* share a harsh and fragile landscape where vast sweeps of desert and arid farmland are split by soaring mountains. Eternal snows and glaciers on the peaks feed huge rivers.

The Soviets did everything on a big scale in the countries they took over. They built enormous dams, and forced the traditional village people to move onto large collective farms. Traditional food plants and animal herds were set aside in favor of cash crops dictated from Moscow. Enormous acreage was planted in cotton, grown for export to fabric mills elsewhere. Poisonous chemicals were applied to the cotton to protect it from insects, and the plants depleted the soil of nutrients. Large-scale irrigation of deserts caused barren salt marshes to spread across the land. The natural wealth of the *Stans* was extracted and taken to Moscow.

Worst of all, the Soviets tested nuclear weapons in Kazakhstan, contaminating the soil and water with radiation that caused illnesses and birth defects that have continued for generations.

The Soviets imported their rigid one-party rule and smothered the press in each of their republics. They stifled Islam, just as they did Christianity and Judaism in other parts of their empire. The Soviets jailed Mullahs, and they jailed or exiled or executed intellectuals who dared to oppose them. The Soviets, having colonized the *Stans*, set their sights on marching farther south into Afghanistan.

It was hard for Meena to understand how anyone could cooperate with the Soviets, but inside the country, collaborators were ready. Some Afghans, especially those who were educated in Russia, looked forward to turning the nation over to Soviet-style communism. The schools, hospitals, and military aid the Soviets held out as rewards looked to them like an improvement over Afghanistan's poverty and ignorance. Some opportunist Afghan Soviet supporters hoped to gain jobs and advancement for themselves, regardless of what was good for the nation.

The Soviet menace seemed so obvious to Meena that she was certain that if only people could be alerted to it, they would wake up and take action to prevent the takeover that was happening.

As the country fell more and more under the sway of Moscow, it was obvious to Meena and Faiz that Afghanistan's crisis would not allow either of them to live quiet lives. In another time, they could have looked forward to her law degree and career; children, a home, his medical practice, and participation together in positive change in their nation. But the times were not normal. Their lives were going to take another course.

6

THE FOUNDING

While her husband practiced medicine and met with his compatriots to discuss the ideas of Mao Zedong, Meena tried to find her own way. It was hard for her to get carried away by abstract political theories when she had to carry heavy buckets of water several times a day. She loved her husband, but she did not want to be his behind-the-scenes supporter. She studied hard at the university, but learning the law became meaningless when the government itself was lawless. More and more people were being arrested for opposition to the regime. The political situation in the country was becoming desperate, and she had no satisfying way to take part.

Meena couldn't stop thinking about the need to do something for women. The wives of men who had been arrested had begun to take their children to the gates of the huge old fortresslike stone prison at the edge of Kabul, trying to get information about their husbands. Meena decided to go there, too, just to talk with the women and show her support. It was the perfect thing for a young law student to do. Why should she wait to finish her studies when women needed her support right then? She wished there were more she could do, but all she had to offer was her sympathy.

She saw her husband's dedication to his organization and the support it gave him for his ideas and actions. Why couldn't there be an organization that would work for women only? Meena knew about women's groups elsewhere in the Muslim world. In Egypt, the socialist-feminist leader Nawal El Saadawi was famous for her outspoken views, and she had been jailed for expressing them.

There were women's charities and women's professional associations in Afghanistan, but a feminist political organization did not exist. Meena dreamed about starting a group that could be supported by ordinary women like her own neighbors and aunts. She asked Faiz what he thought.

"It will be an activist group," she told him, "based on broad principles of unity many women will support." He said he supported her goals, and he encouraged her to try it.

Like many big moments in history, the founding of the first Afghan women's antifundamentalist political organization started small, and with the simplest actions. Meena decided to quietly contact a few women she trusted. She had to be careful. Before the king was overthrown, she could have announced the formation of a women's liberation group, but Kabul was far too dangerous for open organizing by then. No one would have felt safe coming to a public meeting.

Meena talked first to one, then another of her closest friends to discuss her idea. As soon as just one other woman joined her, Meena was not alone. She knew nearly a dozen women who were as ready to act as she was. They were students like her, young women she had known since high school.

A tiny group met over tea, as if they were family members. Meena told them that they could set out to do what women in other nations had done in enormous and powerful movements— to organize themselves for political aims that would benefit women. Their first task, they agreed, was to invite more of their friends to join them.

One day near the end of 1976, Meena went to the home of one of her high school friends to pay a sympathy call. The young woman's mother had died of an illness. The gathering was a *fatihah*—a wake—where, in separate rooms, men and women were talking and praying, weeping and drinking tea.

To Meena's surprise, she saw that her old math and science

teacher was there, in the women's circle around the bereaved girl. Meena and Madame Sadaf embraced in the traditional Afghan way, exchanging three kisses on the cheek—left, right, left. Meena sat down beside Sadaf, who had folded her tall frame onto the *toshak*. The two of them leaned close to talk quietly together. They had not seen each other since Meena's graduation from Malalai. Sadaf was interested in how Meena's studies were going.

"I'm doing well," Meena said. "But what really interests me is trying to do something for the women who are not at the university at all. I want to help the women who are most defenseless, and I don't want to wait to finish my studies to do it."

"I knew you would do great things," Sadaf told her. "I want to encourage you to try."

"May I come to see you at your home?" Meena asked. "I'd like to ask for your advice."

When Sadaf opened her door a few days later to find a woman standing on her doorstep in a *burqa*, it did not occur to her that this was Meena, who usually did not wear even a head scarf.

"Why are you wearing a *burqa*?" Sadaf asked.

"I will explain," Meena told her.

When they were alone, drinking tea, Meena said she was contacting some of her dearest old friends, asking each one to join her in starting a group of women.

"I wore the *burqa* coming here because I want to keep my work secret at first," Meena explained. "Because of the police and the fundamentalists, I have to protect myself and the women I'm visiting. I'm trying to gather a trusted group of friends who can support each other. From now on, you should call me Laila."

Sadaf laughed. "How can you be Laila now? Your name was Meena before." Meena smiled, but she said, "I'm serious. I really don't want my name known. I don't think it's safe. A few women have been meeting for some time to discuss how to help women— not only well-off women, but the poorest women. We are trying to see what we can do. I respect your ideas so much. Will you come and give us your advice?"

Sadaf said yes. She attended her first meeting in early 1977. She and Meena went together to the home of a friend, as if they were making a social visit. There were three other women there. One was another of Sadaf's former students from Malalai. One was a friend of Meena's from the university, and the third was one of Meena's neighbors. Three were young like Meena, and two were older women.

Meena told them she had already done the preliminary work for creating an organization. She said she was meeting secretly with two other small groups. There were eleven women altogether, she told them; but for their protection, she did not think they should meet each other. So many people had disappeared into prisons for opposing the regime, that the women would feel more secure knowing that if one of them were questioned, even if her family were threatened or she were tortured, she would not be able to give the authorities the names of the others.

"I am starting this group the only way I can under the circumstances. Many of you actually do know each other," she told them. "But for safety, I will not tell you who the others are." She asked each of them to choose a false name. "Mine is Laila," she said.

Meena did not invent the idea of structuring an organization in small clandestine groups. People all over the world—regardless of their ideological aims—know this is one way to resist and have a chance to survive under a repressive regime. But in Afghanistan, it was unusual for a group of unrelated women to come together for any purpose. The extended family normally met all needs of Afghan women, who did not have or seek out any other social contacts. Meena pulled her friends beyond their families and into a group with a much wider perspective. This was revolutionary in itself.

Everything depended on each woman's trust in Meena. She was the only one who knew everyone. The force of her personality, the way she showed how much she cared about each member, and the depth of her sincerity and commitment brought the small groups together.

No one knows how she summoned up the courage to take these

first steps. It is certain that she drew upon all that she had ever learned about freedom. Her husband encouraged her. Most of all, she relied on her closest women friends. Their organization was born among a very small circle of women who somehow believed, through the strength of Meena's conviction, that together, against all odds, they could do something.

At their first meetings, they decided on a name for their group. They knew they wanted it to include the word *zan*—women. Meena was adamant, and the others agreed, that they would open the group to women only.

"Who but women will work for women, and only women?" Meena asked. They knew they would be joining in the Muslim women's movement that had already taken hold in Algeria, Iran, Egypt, and other nations.

Meena talked about the political groups she had observed in which women were expected to defer their needs to the "revolution," after which, presumably, women's issues would be addressed. As far as Meena was concerned, that might be never.

"Afghan women are an oppressed group within an oppressed group," she said. "We have different goals than men, and much more ground to gain."

"All the men do is talk, talk, talk, and argue politics!" another woman complained. "I want to be in a group that actually helps people."

"Women," Meena told them, "are an untapped source of great strength. Look at what we accomplish every day, feeding our families, caring for children. If we can come together to act in unison, we can make changes no one has dreamed of."

So *zan* it would be.

They also decided to use the word *inkalab*, Farsi for revolutionary, because any attempt to change the lives of Afghan women would be truly revolutionary.

But what kind of group would it be? They rejected the idea of a political party. They were not trying to take political power, but to influence Afghan society to see women as equal to men. Meena thought their women's organization should be open to ordinary women, mothers, and students, who could contribute whatever time and resources they were able to give. Their name would be *jamiat*, an association.

And so the name was chosen: *Jamiat Zan Inkalab Afghanistan.* The Revolutionary Association of the Women of Afghanistan.

No one remembers when they first began to use the acronym— RAWA—but it was very early. It was easy to say and remember, and easy for foreign supporters to understand. It worked in English, Spanish, and many other languages. So as soon as it was used, it stuck, and became the shorthand name they all used.

Next, the women discussed their founding principles. What did they believe in that they could agree on?

First of all, they agreed to work for democracy, by which they meant the restoration of elections in Afghanistan, and the right to vote for women and men. There had not been an election since the one in which Meena's mothers and father had voted, in 1964.

But it was not enough just to advocate for democracy. They wanted to put it into practice. They would decide everything collectively. They had quite enough of taking orders in their lives, from the government, as well as at home. They wanted to practice democracy and show every member, no matter how young or inexperienced, that she could participate fully in making decisions. They made a commitment to discuss issues until they reached consensus.

Second, they agreed their mission would be to struggle for equality and social justice for women. By that they meant the basic rights of women to education, legal rights, health care, and freedom from poverty and violence.

After much discussion they agreed that religious observance was up to each individual to choose, and should not be dictated by their organization or by any future government of Afghanistan. Theirs would be a nonreligious organization that would advocate a secular government for Afghanistan and religious freedom for all.

Decisions about marriage, work, children, and how to dress were left up to each individual member. Meena knew that her personal life was closely observed by the women around her and that how she lived was part of her message to them.

The fact that she did not stay at home as a wife made her marriage unconventional. All of the women in the founding group were curious about Meena's new husband and what he thought of the project she had taken on. Did he know what she was doing? Women who had not met Faiz called him "the doctor."

"What does the doctor think of RAWA?" they asked her.

"He is my partner," she told them. "When I told him of my plans to establish a feminist women's group, he urged me to do so ahead of everything else—even my studies, and my housework—and devote all of my time and energy to it."

"But does he approve of our work?" one friend asked.

"His support of our work is not only out of respect for me," she said. "He truly shares our goals."

Some of the founders were worried that Dr. Ahmed's party would try to exert a pro-China influence on RAWA.

"If I wanted to join a Maoist party, I would do so," Sadaf said. "But I want our group to stand on its own feet."

Meena promised that they would always remain completely independent. "I want to liberate Afghan women for Afghan women, in the Afghan way. I am a democrat. I have my own mind."

Sadaf laughed, "Yes you do!" The other women smiled, and Meena continued, "My husband knows I have my own views, and he doesn't try to convert me to his ideas. He's happy that I have my own work."

A year had passed since Meena and Faiz had married. Their friend Mowaish inquired about a baby every time she saw Meena. In Afghanistan everyone hopes for a baby in the first year of marriage.

"When will we hold your little one?" Mowaish would tease. But there was no teasing Meena. She did not answer with a bride's demure smile. She replied seriously.

"No. My work is too important. Faiz and I both agree, we want to put off having children." Mowaish could only marvel at their very different kind of marriage, where everything was discussed, and they made decisions together.

In 1977 President Daoud called a sham *Loya Jirga*—a national council—at which handpicked delegates approved a new constitution and elected him president for six more years. Meanwhile, the behind-the-scenes machinations of the U.S.S.R. were eroding Afghanistan's stability day by day.

Throughout 1977, the RAWA women met in their homes to discuss their principles, study women's problems, and think about what they could do. As Meena recruited more members, more small groups were added, and Meena met with them all.

From the beginning, the women scorned the men's political groups that were organized along ethnic lines and ended up warring with each other. They decided they would welcome women of every ethnicity. Regardless of what part of Afghanistan a woman came from, or her tribal origin, she could join if she supported their principles.

Meena, whose political awareness had begun with her revulsion for discrimination against Hazaras like her neighbor Shama, stressed tolerance for each other's differences. The RAWA women hoped that perhaps women, who had so much in common as wives and mothers, could come together across tribal lines. From the beginning, they made recruitment of minority women a priority.

They pooled their resources to help meet each other's needs. They shared food and gave each other outgrown clothes for their children. They learned how to help each other survive. They also talked about their personal affairs. If a woman was mistreated, at home the group would talk about how she could avoid that in the future.

They even helped each other make decisions about marriage. If a member's family arranged her marriage, she also asked for the group's approval, not just her family's. She would not accept the marriage unless the husband would agree that she could continue her feminist work.

Nothing a woman needed to talk about was taboo. This was another way RAWA became stronger than the male political groups.

The women forged intimate emotional bonds. During these early meetings Meena talked about having seen her father abuse her mothers, and confessed that her grandmother also was beaten by her grandfather. Often, the women cried during their meetings, telling about the violence they had witnessed. Meena did not try to hide her sadness from her friends.

In those early days, RAWA's activity was minimal. Mostly, they just had meetings where they got to know and trust each other. Often, all of the RAWA groups read and discussed the same book. One of their favorite authors was the Russian novelist Maxim Gorky, who wrote several compelling novels about the stifled lives of poor women, which were translated into Farsi and widely available in Afghanistan. It was Gorky who wrote, "Only mothers can think of the future, because they give birth to it in their children."

The core group around Meena was growing into a close circle of friends. But how to grow beyond their small beginnings? All of them were surrounded in their neighborhoods, and even in their own extended families, with daily examples of the oppression of women. To every meeting they brought tales of suffering: young girls forced into far-too-early marriages, beaten, forced to leave school, or even raped and forced to marry the rapist. What could they do?

As educated women, they knew one way to reach out to their less fortunate sisters: They could teach them to read. Only 8 percent of girls in the nation were enrolled in primary school. The constitution granted girls the right to education, but that meant nothing in places where there were no schools, no teachers, and girls were not allowed out of their homes. Meena suggested that they go to rural villages near Kabul where members of the group had relatives or friends and start free weekly literacy classes.

Roya was a typical illiterate woman. Though her husband was a teacher, he felt no need to teach his young wife how to read. Meena met Roya through a friend in her neighborhood and liked her right away. Roya was a down-to-earth peasant woman with hennaed red hair, poor teeth, expressive full lips, and startlingly green eyes. She was from a tiny village and had moved to Kabul after her marriage. Roya was the kind of woman Meena had hoped to include in RAWA—uneducated but tough and wise. She and her husband were both critical of the Daoud regime, and Meena invited her to join a literacy class.

Once Meena trusted Roya, she asked her if she could hold the class at her home. Roya was proud to have the group come. Usually Meena taught the class herself, but sometimes someone else would come to teach. They moved Roya's class from home to home that first year. Roya couldn't always go, and she was not a fast learner, but it meant a great deal to her to know Meena and the others.

Meena knew that literacy alone would not free women. She saw RAWA's classes as a way to show women who could not imagine different lives that they might have some new options.

"We have to start with basic literacy," Meena said, "but we cannot stop at that. We have to show them that they are not inferior, that they do not have to obey men, or an unjust government."

The women in RAWA's small groups were making contacts and friendships with people outside of the university, and even outside Kabul. They were finding out that women could cross the class and cultural lines that had divided townspeople from peasants for generations. After all, women always had something in common— husbands, children, and the edicts of mothers-in-law.

RAWA recruited new members in Herat, Jalalabad, and Mazar-e Sharif, cities where there were schools for girls who were receptive to their ideas.

If they were idealistic about how easy it might be to raise the consciousness of illiterate women, their practical experiences teaching literacy classes soon woke them up to the reality. Their students faced huge obstacles to freedom. Fathers forbade them to study; husbands punished them for reading. RAWA's literacy teachers soon learned what a long road lay ahead of them on their journey to bring knowledge to the mass of Afghan women.

They had the support of each other to lean on, though, and in their small groups they worked out strategies for helping their students. At their weekly meetings, RAWA members gave reports on the literacy classes, their plans for the coming week, new recruits, and volunteers. No matter how slowly the group was growing, or how frustrating their attempts to change the mind-set of women, Meena encouraged them with her long-range view of what they were attempting to do.

Sadaf gave the younger women this advice: "In a society like Afghanistan, where women are still under the oppression of men, change cannot be made in a short time. We know that this will not take one or two years, but decades. We have to build in a way that will last."

Outside the capital, women were rarely seen traveling unaccompanied by men. Conservative Islam custom requires a woman to be with a *mahrahm*—a close male relative—whenever she is outside the family compound. RAWA members were much safer with a man escorting them. From nearly the beginning, they had male supporters who were not threatened by the idea of women's equality. These husbands, brothers, cousins, or sons agreed with RAWA's aims and played essential roles as drivers and protectors.

"Lots of men would join RAWA," Meena joked, "if we were not a women's organization."

Mainly, their organization grew by word of mouth. Women invited their friends and relatives to come to a meeting. But soon they began to write and distribute flyers—called *shabnameh*—literally, night letters. The flyers were not for recruitment, but to spread opposition to the regime. There never was a time when RAWA felt safe to organize openly.

Always, the age-old women's culture of Afghanistan that oppressed them also sustained them. Though the separation of the sexes stifled women who wanted to move into work and learning, it also meant that women traditionally spent long hours together. A group of men meeting together might look suspicious, but women gathering to talk was as normal as *naan*. RAWA turned every common women's custom into a tool of liberation. Every woman walked out at dawn or dusk to the *hamom*, the communal baths, carrying a change of clean clothes with her. The bath bundles of a few women concealed books and leaflets.

The *burqa*, which they as modern women had rejected, they adopted for its many uses in their clandestine work. Under their *burqas*, they were not only anonymous, but they appeared to be their own opposites: They looked like the most conservative and obedient of women, not like the rebels they were. The *burqa* also covered whatever contraband they needed to carry. And when they could not hold back their tears, they picked up the hated but ample cloth of the *burqa* and used it to wipe their eyes.

Meena was in her second year at the university, but more and more of her time was taken up by the demands of RAWA. The campus was in continuous uproar over politics. The pro-Soviet parties, *Khalq* and *Parcham*, had grown much larger and dangerously militant. They were active not only at the university and colleges, but also in the military, the schools, and many government departments. It was increasingly dangerous for anyone opposed to them to speak out or to meet.

Meena's education was something she had worked for since she was a young girl. But her work with RAWA had become much more important than her studies, and she decided to leave the university. Meena told Faiz that she wanted to devote herself to RAWA full-time.

He nodded. "It will take all of your time and effort," he said.

"This will be a personal sacrifice for both of us," she said. "I want us to decide it together."

Faiz kissed her. "I give you my full support," he said.

Meena and Faiz could still hope for the life they had imagined, but for now the situation was so urgent, they would put their life as a couple on hold. The future of Afghanistan was more important to them than any other concern. More important even than time to be alone together.

Married just a year, they hoped that someday there would be a time for them. But it could not be now.

7

GROWING
DANGER

Early on the morning of Valentine's Day, 1978, the U.S. ambassador to Afghanistan was hijacked in his limousine by men wearing the police uniforms of the Afghan government. They took Ambassador Adolph Dubs to a room in the downtown Kabul Hotel and held him hostage. It seemed that perhaps the kidnappers were not really police, because they demanded that the government release Islamic militant prisoners. Afghan government troops surrounded the hotel, climbed onto nearby rooftops, and crept into the corridor outside the room.

U.S. embassy staff sped to the scene and tried to take control of the confused situation. They begged the representatives of Daoud's government to order their troops not to shoot the kidnappers, but to try to negotiate with them. Suddenly, however, the troops opened fire, filling the hotel room with bullets. Ambassador Dubs was killed, and so was one of the kidnappers. The rest escaped. No one ever determined who the hijackers were, or what the Daoud regime's involvement in the kidnapping was.

The result was further U.S. disengagement from Afghanistan. Four thousand Americans were living in Kabul, many of them teaching at the University or working in aid projects. They began to withdraw.

Daoud's efforts to get help dealing with the increasing Soviet control in Afghanistan had come too late. He had traveled to Iran,

Pakistan, and Saudi Arabia to ask for development aid. His former pro-Soviet allies, many of them members of the Afghan army who had been trained in the Soviet Union, finally moved against him.

The Muslim holy day is Friday, and the weekend in Afghanistan begins with a half day of work on Thursdays. On the afternoon of Thursday, April 27, 1978, when government workers and military officers had left their offices, men loyal to the People's Democratic Party of Afghanistan (PDPA)—the coalition of the two feuding pro-Soviet parties, *Khalq* and *Parcham*—took over the Ministry of Defense in Kabul and the offices of the national radio station, Radio Afghanistan. Their leader was Nur Mohammed Taraki. They broadcast a short announcement:

"For the first time in the history of Afghanistan, the last remnants of monarchy, tyranny, despotism, and power . . . has (sic) ended, and all powers of the state are in the hands of the people of Afghanistan. The power rests fully with the Revolutionary Council of the Armed Forces."

For anyone listening, this was chilling news. No one knew who the Revolutionary Council of the Armed Forces were.

Shortly, another statement was broadcast:

"Dear compatriots! Your popular state, which is in the hands of the Revolutionary Council, informs you that every antirevolutionary element who would venture to defy the instruction and rulings of the Revolutionary Council will be delivered immediately to the revolutionary military centers."

The whole nation held its breath. In their homes, the hearts of the women of RAWA skipped beats. By the end of the weekend the news had spread: Prince Daoud had been murdered, along with his whole family and his corps of bodyguards. In Kabul, some two thousand other people close to Daoud had also been killed.

The nightmare that had been announced came true. A faction of the army, soldiers who had been trained in the Soviet Union, spread out across the cities and towns arresting anyone they even suspected of not supporting them. Many of the soldiers were the same men who had helped Daoud overthrow the king six years before. Now they were hunting new victims. Simply being a member of the upper classes could mean arrest or death. Thousands were taken to the military bases.

Professors, lawyers, doctors, writers, teachers—anyone who had been in a political party other than *Parcham* or *Khalq was* no longer safe, even in their homes.

Meena and Faiz took refuge with friends. They also tried to protect, if possible, their best friends, Mowaish and Shohib. Though Shohib was in the army, he refused to go along with what was happening. He was arrested and thrown into prison. Mowaish's brothers were also taken away. Within days, the news came that Mowaish's brothers had all been summarily executed. There was no news of Mowaish's husband, Shohib. He had simply disappeared. As hard as they tried, Meena and Faiz could not find out where he was or what had happened to him.

Meena and Faiz had to assume the police were looking for Faiz, too. It was too dangerous for him to go to see Mowaish and her daughters, in case the police were watching their house. Meena put on her *burqa*, and summoning all of her courage, made her way to Mowaish's house. She found Mowaish and the girls sitting in darkness, collapsed in grief. The oldest daughter told Meena what had happened.

"We were all at home, my parents and me and the other kids, when there was a knock. It was soldiers at the door. They said Father had to come with them. He changed his shoes and got his coat. He didn't say a word. He took most of the money out of his wallet and handed it to me. He told me to take care of my mother, and he kissed me. Then he walked out with them. I'll never forget how brave he was."

Meena wept with the whole family, holding Mowaish in her arms.

Faiz had to go into hiding. He could no longer go to his office or meet openly with his political allies. He could not visit his family members. He began to move from house to house, staying with trusted friends or relatives. Meena was afraid she would lead the soldiers to him. She, too, moved from place to place, seeing Faiz only at prearranged meetings in houses where they felt safe.

The terrible times forced RAWA to pull together and become stronger. Many members had lost close male relatives. Meena was on the move constantly in her *burqa*, visiting her shocked and bereaved friends.

The new regime unfurled a new flag, changing the color from Islamic green to communist red. Almost from the start, the regime was bitterly divided into its two factions, *Parcham* and *Khalq*. A few short months after they seized power, the leader, Taraki, was assassinated. Hazifullah Amin took over. Afghanistan was descending into chaos.

Between April and September 1978, thousands of Afghans— some estimates are as high as a hundred thousand—disappeared. Most of them were killed. In the face of this level of repression, an organization for women's rights alone made no sense. RAWA had to broaden its mission to freedom for the nation.

Meena told Sadaf, "Today, we are an organization of women struggling for the liberation of women *and* Afghanistan."

In September 1978, the regime arrested the head of the family that had lived next door when Meena and Faiz first married. They were the neighbors who had let Meena draw water from their well. Meena and Faiz had moved from that house when the repression began, but when Meena heard of the father's arrest, she went back to see them.

Asifa, the thirteen-year-old niece of the man who had been arrested, was grateful for Meena's concern. Asifa was pretty and a little plump, and wore her fine black hair cut short. She was a serious, thoughtful girl who reminded Meena of herself as a teenager. Weeping, Asifa confided that her father had also disappeared, at the same time her uncle had been arrested.

She was holding Meena's hand in her two hands. She said, "Even some of our closest relatives and friends haven't come to the house because they're afraid. Our neighbors pretend they don't know us. Thank you so much for being here."

At first, they didn't say anything political to each other. Meena did not tell Asifa or her aunt about RAWA. Asifa was still going to school, and students could be pressured and questioned—it was not safe for them to know secrets.

A few months later, Asifa's cousin was also arrested. He was a student at the Polytechnic. Forty-eight students there were arrested at the same time. The people who were arrested, including Asifa's cousin, were not given trials. They just disappeared. Intellectuals were being picked up randomly, regardless of their political affiliations.

Meena and Asifa grew closer, and began to trust each other. They talked about their shared hatred for the pro-Soviet puppet regime. Meena told Asifa's aunt that she had accompanied women to the jails, and she volunteered to go with her to try to find her husband and son.

Every day off, on Fridays, the women made the rounds of the jails: Puli-Charkhi, Dehmazang. They joined the lines of women going from jail to jail, trying to find out what had happened to their loved ones.

Meena confided to Asifa, "I met a woman who sent her husband a letter and a little bit of bread. The husband sent the bread back out to his wife, for her to feed to their children."

Meanwhile, people began to protest the regime in every part of the nation. Armed uprisings began in the rural areas and spread to cities. In Herat, attacks on Soviet technicians and their families were quelled when the new pro-Soviet puppet regime bombed the city, killing thousands. Afghan soldiers then defected from the U.S.S.R.'s puppet government and formed a guerrilla army in Herat under Commander Ishmail Khan. Armed resistance spread to other cities and across the nation.

The *Khalq* announced "reforms" without even a nod to democratic process or discussion. They mandated land distribution to the poor; but the regime had little control in rural areas, and the people simply ignored the edicts from Kabul. Soon, though, the government sent officials throughout the country to strip landlords of their property and hand out five-acre plots to peasants. Large extended families of former landholders fled into exile or took refuge with relatives in the cities.

Compulsory Marxist education was announced for both boys and girls. Most families were offended and frightened by the prospect of their daughters attending school alongside boys and men. The *Khalq* gave lip service to women's liberation. They prohibited marriage until the age of eighteen and drastically reduced the "prices" of brides.

These were measures that feminists would normally support, but Meena knew they would never be accepted when forcibly imposed by foreigners, especially foreigners who at the same time were enslaving the entire populace and destroying the fabric of ancient traditions.

The fact that the *Khalq* preached advances for women only made RAWA's task of educating people to accept a wider role for women harder. Already, the women of RAWA had to answer false accusations from conservatives that they were communists or "un-Islamic" for wanting a wider role for women. Now they had to dissociate themselves from the puppet "Marxists," while still defending their feminist principles.

Meena's early caution now seemed prescient. She had built RAWA's networks as close circles of trust from the beginning— something that might have seemed overly careful at first, but which served to keep RAWA alive through a time when secrecy was a matter of life or death.

Somehow, the police discovered that one of RAWA's literacy classes had met at Roya's home. As a result, Roya's house was ransacked and her husband was arrested. Roya narrowly escaped being arrested herself. She fled Kabul and made her way to Jalalabad, where she stayed for some months with relatives.

When she returned to Kabul alone, wearing a *burqa*, she found Meena, who by then also wore a *burqa* wherever she went. RAWA found out that the police had no official warrant for Roya's arrest. Nervously, she went to visit her husband in the prison. When she was not arrested, Meena asked her to go back to the prison regularly and try to smuggle messages to prisoners. "It's important that we try to let them know what's happening outside," Meena told her, and Roya agreed.

Roya taped messages to her stockings, or hid them in her hair. Meena came up with a new idea: "Let's pretend your fingers have been cut or burned and tape the message under a bandage."

"I don't think that's going to work," Roya cautioned.

Meena was sure it would.

"Okay, let's try an experiment," Roya said. "I'll bandage my hand, but I won't put anything under the tape."

When she went into the prison, a guard roughly tore off Roya's bandage. "You're not hurt!" he accused her. "Why are you lying?" he demanded angrily.

"See?" Roya teased Meena when she got back. "I was the one who was right that time!"

The two friends had to laugh, even if it was just to keep from crying.

The *Khalq* government signed a new peace treaty with the U.S.S.R. in December, 1978. Immediately, the Soviets sent military "advisors," who were really soldiers, into Afghanistan to help the *Khalq* army suppress any resistance from the people. That same month, Meena realized she was pregnant.

8

TORN APART

Meena's spirit rebelled against bringing a child into the world of chaos that was Afghanistan. She and Faiz no longer even had a home. A child was impossible, unless she completely abandoned her work and lived in anonymous seclusion somewhere. Her husband, hunted by the murderous *Khalq* regime, would never be able to work and care for a family normally—at least not until peace and stability came to Afghanistan, and that seemed like a far-off dream.

Despairing, Faiz and Meena sought out Mowaish. They arranged a secret meeting at the home of friends and confided in her. They asked her advice, as a mother and older woman. An abortion was difficult to obtain, but it was an option, through some of Faiz's medical friends.

Mowaish was alone. After months of searching and praying for her husband, Shohib, she had finally been told that he had died in prison of illness. She was struggling to support her daughters. Mowaish had so few resources, at first she could hardly think what to tell Meena and Faiz.

She loved them both so much that the thought of a child born from these two wonderful people softened her heart. Mowaish, who had lost so much, could not bear to let go of another precious life. She hardly hesitated before she begged Meena to bear the baby and place it in her care.

Meena and Faiz knew Mowaish was a wonderful mother. But Meena was torn with indecision. How could she be certain that Mowaish could care for another child? And how could Meena carry a child within her and give it up, even to a dear and trusted friend? To Mowaish, and to Meena's mother and sisters, motherhood was an Afghan woman's destiny. But Meena had not wanted to give birth.

"What can I do?" she agonized. "A baby will hold back my work. It will end my work for Afghanistan." She delayed making a final decision.

Meena often took refuge with her old teacher Sadaf. She would knock on Sadaf's door after dark, wash herself and her clothes, sleep, and get up at dawn to go on her way.

Sadaf always asked her, "How's the doctor?"

Sometimes Meena answered, "I saw him last night, and he's doing fine." More often she said, "I don't know."

When Meena told Sadaf she was expecting, Sadaf burst out laughing, "I don't know when you've had time to get pregnant!"

Meena grinned.

Sadaf and Meena had long talks about the pregnancy. Meena had heard that the police sometimes tortured the children of political parents in front of them to force them to betray their friends. She asked Sadaf, "How can I bring a child into a world where such a thing can happen?"

But Sadaf was overjoyed by the thought of the baby. So many were dying all around them, to Sadaf, it was time for new life to be born. She thought Meena should go through with the pregnancy for the sake of the child and also for Mowaish, who truly wanted to be its foster mother.

Faiz left the final decision to Meena. In the end, she put her faith in her mother, sisters, and friends, and bowed to their wishes. She agreed to have the baby and allow Mowaish to care for it until a time when she could do so herself. Everyone knew that time might never come.

The events in Iran made any stable future for Afghanistan look impossible. In January 1979, the Shah was forced to leave the country. His brutal rule was replaced by the ultrafanatic regime of the Ayatollah Khomeini. Many saw this change as a reaction to the years of oppression Iranians had suffered at the hands of the Shah's secret police, SAVAK.

Most moderate, secular, and democratic-minded Iranians had long since been eliminated—murdered or forced into exile. The corruption, decadence, and brutality that had marked life under the Shah were blamed on his ally, the United States, and Iranians' anti-American reactions swept the Ayatollah Khomeini into power.

The establishment of the new Islamic regime had a devastating effect on women. Overnight, women were removed from the workplace. Schools were immediately segregated by gender, and childcare centers were closed. Women were barred from studying engineering, architecture, and many other subjects at the universities. Both abortion and birth control were banned. The Mullahs announced that the place for women was in the home, and they lowered the marriage age to thirteen. Thousands were executed on charges of being "anti-Islamic."

To Meena, the Iranian revolution was a chilling warning of what could happen in Afghanistan if RAWA failed to keep feminist and democratic ideas alive. Pregnant or not, she had to work harder than ever. At some point in the early summer of 1979, the women of RAWA inevitably realized Meena was pregnant. Afghan reserve about such matters prevented many of them from asking her about it; but all of them worried, because they hardly saw her eat. She would take just a little bread, or some potatoes. Too often she gave her food away to hungry children in the street.

Meena continued her work throughout the pregnancy, an action which in Afghanistan was unprecedented. "I am not paralyzed," she insisted. "It's a myth perpetrated by men that a pregnant woman is incapable of doing anything at all. I want to prove in practice that this simply is not true."

As her pregnancy progressed, Afghanistan grew more and more

unstable. What kind of world was Meena's baby going to be born into?

Next door in Iran, militants held fifty Americans hostage inside the U.S. embassy. Faced with the instability of the entire region in July 1979, President Jimmy Carter okayed secret aid to the opponents of the pro-Soviet regime in Afghanistan. U.S. Secretary of State Brzezinski predicted that the Soviets might be induced to invade Afghanistan, and then be drawn into a war that would allow the U.S. to strike into the "soft underbelly" of the U.S.S.R. After its own defeat in Vietnam, the United States began to see Afghanistan as a way to "give the Soviets their Vietnam."

Toward the end of her pregnancy, Meena was worn-out. One very hot summer day, near noon, she arrived at the home of one of RAWA's elderly supporters. She asked for something to eat, and the older lady went into the kitchen to prepare a meal for her. Meena followed her and insisted on helping as usual. While she ate, she explained that some families had arrived in Kabul from the country to seek medical treatment, and they needed places to stay, mattresses to sleep on, and dishes. The older woman told Meena to send a cart to take anything they needed from her house. She offered to send her daughter to help the refugees get settled.

Thanking her, Meena suddenly burst into tears of gratitude and sheer exhaustion. She told the woman, "Without your support and the support of so many women like you, we cannot possibly win the war." Meena hugged the woman, who told her she regretted being too old to have the honor of working with her more. Meena replied, "I am the one who is honored."

Throughout her pregnancy, Meena's husband was under extreme pressure. The "Glorious Revolution" that had taken power unleashed its reign of terror on all "counterrevolutionary elements," and activists on both the right and the left were hunted down, arrested, and tortured. This included Faiz's Maoist *Sholayis* as well as the Islamist fanatics. Many on both sides were executed. People were taken away by Afghan functionaries under the direction of agents of the KGB, the Soviet secret police. Very quickly, the arrests spread beyond the known revolutionary groups to teachers, doctors, and business owners.

All this was done in the name of the "People's Democracy" and "the end of the exploitation of man by man." These were slogans the *Sholayis* had used themselves, and the fact that such words were now used to justify the deaths of many of their members made their losses all the more bitter.

All over Kabul, soldiers and police broke down doors and ransacked homes, destroying furniture, even bayoneting mattresses, searching for incriminating papers or books.

August 5, 1979, was the darkest day in Meena's young life. The desperate remnants of Faiz's Maoist party joined with a small group of leftist army officers in an attempt to overthrow the *Khalq* regime. Their hope was to oust the government and replace it with a group that would break ties to the U.S.S.R. Fighting broke out at the Bala Hissar army garrison in Kabul.

Meena got the news that the coup attempt was under way just as she went into labor. She did not think Faiz was directly involved, but she did not know where he was. Frantic with worry, she waited where she was, at the home of friends, hoping Faiz would come. She was terrified he had been hurt or arrested.

Her labor was progressing, but she was afraid to go to the hospital because she was certain the police would be looking for her, too. What if they found her at the hospital and arrested her? Finally, overcome by labor pains, and afraid to deliver her baby without a doctor, Meena went to the hospital at eight in the morning, accompanied by one of her younger sisters. She gave a false name to the nurses.

Meena was twenty-two. She had never seen a birth, and was not sure what to expect. Her unmarried sister was not much help. All Meena could think of was Faiz. If the coup succeeded, the puppet government would be gone. If it failed, Faiz might be killed; and the police could come for Meena, too, at any moment.

Labor contractions took over, and she felt utterly unsafe. For these hours she was completely vulnerable, unable to flee or even to know what was happening outside in the city. The child inside of her had been her companion, its stirrings a secret comfort as Meena, often alone, traversed Kabul on her clandestine errands. When she found a place to lie down alone at night, sheltered by sympathetic friends, but without her husband beside her, she felt her child's movements as her only solace. Now, she and her baby would be separated, perhaps forever. After long hours of terrible pain, a vaginal incision had to be made to allow the baby's head to emerge.

Meena looked at her perfect baby daughter with a mixture of wonder and despair. If she were arrested later that night, she could not imagine what would become of her baby. Thinking a name was perhaps all she would ever be able to give her, Meena told her sister she wanted to name her Anosha—Immortal.

"Where are the baby clothes?" the nurse asked.

"I forgot to bring them," Meena answered.

In reality, she had no clothes for her newborn daughter. As soon as the nurse left the room, Meena got up. She was exhausted and in pain from the newly sewn stitches, but the longer she stayed in the hospital, the more likely it was that her identity would be discovered and she would be arrested.

Her sister helped her. They pulled the sheet from the bed and wrapped the one-hour-old baby girl in it. Meena put on her *burqa* and, with her sister, evaded the nurses, and slipped out of the hospital with her daughter in her arms, into the dangerous streets of Kabul.

Meena had to get to Mowaish, but she was afraid to approach Mowaish's neighborhood. She was terrified that the police were watching for her. If she were arrested, she had no idea what would become of her daughter. Desperate to find a safe place for her, she went to a house where several young RAWA women were living.

Distraught, she asked the girls to keep the baby for her. She could not tell them Mowaish was going to be the baby's foster mother—no one was supposed to know. She had to leave the baby until she could contact Mowaish herself. As she placed the baby in the arms of one of the girls, Meena felt nothing but anguish. Her foreboding about her pregnancy had come true in a more horrible way than she could have imagined. There was no joy in her child's birth, only fear.

She fled, leaving her baby, to seek news of Faiz. She found out the mutiny had not lasted the night. Soldiers loyal to the Soviets savagely crushed the rebels and killed most of them. Just as she had feared, police were searching the city for anyone connected to the uprising.

In the following days, Meena was able to learn that Faiz was alive, but had been arrested in the police crackdown after the coup attempt. Desperately, she started contacting everyone she could think of who might help her to gain his release.

Days passed, but the RAWA girls did not hear from Meena. They knew little about caring for a baby, and they had nothing to feed her. They were afraid to venture out into the streets to get milk or seek help. They desperately tried to feed her boiled water. They had no sugar, so they tried dissolving hard candies in the water to sweeten it. Mowaish had no way of knowing any of this was happening.

After several days Meena was at last able to go back and get her baby, but she could only keep her long enough to feed her a few times.

The next afternoon, Mowaish stepped out of her house to go to a shop, and when she returned, one of her daughters said, "Mother, Meena left this baby." A tiny girl lay on the *toshak* wrapped in a blanket. By then, she was several days old, weak, and had serious diarrhea.

Mowaish rushed out to buy formula. She had baby clothes left from her youngest, and she got those and dressed the baby. Mowaish and her daughters had all been nearly destroyed by the loss of Shohib and Mowaish's three brothers. Their house had been dark and silent with grief. Now, they gathered around the sickly baby girl who filled the house with new life and let them forget their pain.

During the first two months of her baby's life, Meena was focused on trying to contact anyone who could help her to save Faiz's life and free him. The authorities were not able to connect him to the coup attempt. Nevertheless, they tortured him. At last, he managed to escape from prison with the help of a guard who knew him as a doctor. He and Meena were reunited in a safe place for only a few days. For the first time, he saw their baby girl.

The Maoist groups were never large enough to be an important factor in Afghanistan's struggle for freedom, but at least they could say they had done their best to try to prevent the disaster that was rolling over its people.

It was clear to Meena and Faiz that he could no longer live safely in Kabul. He left quickly for Pakistan, with no idea when he would be reunited with his wife and his daughter, or how. He made his way to Peshawar, where hundreds of thousands of Afghans had sought refuge.

Meena stayed behind in Kabul. RAWA needed her now more than ever, and her baby seemed safe with Mowaish. Meena saw her daughter once or twice a month, but forced herself to let Mowaish be her mother. To everyone's relief, after three months, the resilient baby girl was thriving. Mowaish proudly showed her off when Meena visited.

It was terrible for Mowaish to see Meena's poor state of health. Meena had no stable place to stay, and the old effects of typhoid fever plagued her. Her legs ached constantly during the cold winter of 1979–80. Her seizures were more frequent when she was exhausted. She was so busy and on the run that she rarely ate well, and her skin, always delicate, was chafed and raw.

There were by then so many destitute widows in Kabul that many had no choice but to beg on the streets. Once, while walking alone, Meena had a seizure. When she woke up, she found that a passerby, thinking she was a beggar, had put some money into her hand.

Roya had worked with Meena throughout the pregnancy, but she did not see Meena for a while, and then, when they met again,

Meena was no longer pregnant. In Afghanistan that winter, it was too dangerous to ask questions. Roya longed to talk about personal things with this young woman she had come to love, but it was safer for both of them that she not know. Roya had never met Meena's husband and knew nothing about him. So she never asked Meena about her baby—what sex it was, or where it was. They had work to do, smuggling leaflets.

Large groups of women continued to gather at Puli-Charkhi Prison to demand news of their jailed sons, brothers, husbands, and fathers. The police dispersed one of the demonstrations with gunfire. Meena rushed to help RAWA print and distribute thousands of flyers publicizing the government's violent response to the peaceful gathering. By the fall of 1979, twelve thousand political prisoners were being held by the regime in Kabul alone. Asifa, the niece of Meena's former neighbors, knew that her father, uncle, and cousin were among them.

Finally, in October 1979, the Interior Ministry announced that a list of prisoners would be released. Meena went with fourteen-year-old Asifa and thousands of others to the prison gate. Instead of a list of prisoners, the people were given a list of the thirteen thousand people the government had executed in Kabul alone. Meena and Asifa sat together on the ground, running their fingers down the long list of the dead, and wept. Asifa's father's name was on the list, and her cousin's. Meena cried with Asifa as if she were a member of her family.

Asifa asked, "Why did they even make such a list? Just to be cruel? They must have gotten sick of so many women demonstrating."

Meena took Asifa back home and helped with the terrible task of telling her mother the unbearable news. When Meena left, Asifa asked her to come back to see her again whenever she could.

One evening, Meena appeared at Asifa's door and asked to stay the night. She and Asifa lay down in the same room. For hours Asifa asked questions, and Meena talked to her. Meena explained, "The *Khalq* killed your father and all of the others because they are committing genocide against all intellectuals—old and young. They are trying to kill ideas, and that is why they slaughtered thirteen thousand innocent, freedom-loving people. We cannot allow your father's death to be in vain."

Meena and Asifa talked nearly all night. Meena talked to Asifa about Shama, the Hazara servant girl who lived next door to her family when she was Asifa's age. She said she didn't want Afghan women to suffer that way. And she told Asifa about reading the life story of Ashraf Dihquany, the Iranian woman who was a freedom fighter. She said she didn't share Ashraf's political views, but that Asifa must be inspired by Ashraf's determination to try to be a savior of her nation.

Meena went to Mowaish's house whenever she could, or whenever she could bear it, to see her baby girl. Inevitably, there was some tension between mother and foster mother. The day the baby's first tooth came in, Meena happened to come to see her. Mowaish and her daughters were all very happy, because in Afghanistan, a baby's first tooth is an occasion to celebrate. Meena stayed only a few minutes. She took the baby's hand, kissed it, grabbed her *burqa*, and left the house in a hurry.

The next time she came back, Mowaish said to her, "We were all so happy about her tooth, and we thought you'd be happy, too. But you were indifferent."

Meena started to cry, and said, "How can you think I'm not interested in her? I act the way I do toward her out of love, because I know if she gets too used to me, it will be too hard on her. You know that if people notice she is mine, she could be in danger. It doesn't mean I don't care about my child! I do, but my work must come first."

Meena's old math teacher Sadaf saw Meena's baby for the first time when she was a few months old. Meena came to Sadaf's house, and another member brought the baby there to meet Meena.

It was obvious to Sadaf the baby was not bonded to Meena as her mother. To Sadaf, it seemed strange, but she knew Meena had no choice but to protect the baby and herself from becoming close. Sadaf, holding the chubby baby, couldn't help saying, "Meena, you must miss her so much. She's so beautiful."

Meena smiled sadly and nodded, but all she said was, "The foster mother is such a wonderful mother. The foster mother is better for this baby."

Whenever Sadaf asked about the baby, Meena gave the same answers she used to give when she was asked about Faiz. Sometimes she said, "I just saw her, and she is well." Sometimes she said sadly, "I don't know."

On December 27, 1979, the voice of Babrak Karmal, the exiled leader of the *Parcham* party, was heard on the radio. He announced that he was broadcasting from inside Afghanistan, but he was actually at a radio station located in Tajikistan, the Soviet Republic just north of the Afghan border. He proclaimed "a new stage of the Glorious Revolution."

At the same hour, Babrak Karmal's archenemy, President Hazifullah Amin was poisoned by Soviet guards in his Kabul palace. As Amin lay dying, fifty thousand Soviet soldiers poured into Afghanistan. Babrak Karmal rode into Afghanistan at the head of a line of Soviet tanks.

Meena's baby was only a little over four months old. Mowaish held her in her arms as she and her daughters stood with thousands of other people, silently watching the Soviet tanks roll into Kabul. Every person in the crowd now had a choice to make: to try to survive this invasion quietly, or to fight back.

9

UNDERGROUND

In January 1980, in an effort to gain popular support, the Soviet puppet government headed by Babrak Karmal announced there would be a release of prisoners. Again, a huge crowd of women went to the gates of Puli-Charkhi Prison, expecting thousands of their men to walk out through them. The gates opened, but only 150 men emerged. The gates slammed shut again.

The women rioted, throwing stones and screaming, and succeeded in forcing the gates open. Inside, they discovered a pile of corpses.

Afterward, Meena went to Asifa's house. As soon as she got inside, she fainted. Asifa ran for water and sat gently sponging Meena's face.

When Meena could speak, she said, "I just visited a woman whose son was killed in Puli-Charkhi Prison. Her screams and the look of pain on her face were so terrible." Meena could hardly stop crying. Over and over she told Asifa, "I'll never forget this. Never."

She was utterly exhausted. That night she stayed with Asifa, and she trembled in her sleep the entire night.

In March 1980, Sadaf's home was searched by the police. They found nothing, but they took her to jail and questioned her for four hours. She was terrified, but did not tell them anything, and they let her go. She did not know why they suspected her, a high school math teacher.

Even after that, Sadaf continued to help write and distribute RAWA's leaflets. One of them was found by a girl named Yelda, a petite, bright-eyed fourteen-year-old, who wore round eyeglasses and long brown braids. She was in the bathroom at the Aisha Durrani High School for girls when she saw the leaflet. Yelda looked around to check that no one was watching as she reached out to pick up the piece of paper. It called on students to come to a public demonstration against the Soviets.

The demonstration was on a Friday when there was no school. Yelda had no one to go with her. She left her family's home all alone, hoping no one she knew would see her, or if they did, that they wouldn't tell other students or teachers she had been there. There were collaborators and spies everywhere.

Thousands of students came to the center of the city, holding up signs demanding democracy. Yelda didn't know anyone, so she joined in with some other girls her age. When the police came, Yelda ran away through back alleys. Before she could get on a bus to go home, she had to walk slowly to calm down so that she wouldn't give herself away to the other passengers by breathing hard. After she got off the bus, she had to make sure she wasn't followed as she walked home. If her activities caused her family to be suspected of anti-Soviet activities, her home could be raided and Yelda or her parents could "disappear."

Back at school, Yelda watched carefully, looking for girls she thought might also be against the Soviets. The school had been reorganized along Soviet lines. The principal and teachers were forced to promote pro-Soviet slogans and fly the new Afghan flag with the green stripe replaced by red. Girls who volunteered to participate in pro-Soviet activities were rewarded. Yelda refused to participate in as many of these "patriotic" games, clubs, marches, and trips as she could without arousing too much suspicion. She made excuses, saying she was sick, or had to go home to help her mother. She noticed two other girls who also hung back, and they noticed her. The three of them made friends, but they were all too afraid to say anything political to each other.

But then disaster struck Yelda's family. One of her brothers was arrested and held in jail. The other two girls heard about what had happened, and they saw Yelda's despair. They approached her in the schoolyard and spoke to her privately. They told her they were working with RAWA, and invited her to join.

Now at least Yelda had friends who understood, and she was pleased that there was something she could do. All through the rest of tenth grade, Yelda worked for RAWA, distributing leaflets and carefully recruiting other girls to join. A RAWA member would bring leaflets to Yelda's home or pass them to her at school when no one was looking. If she had to carry leaflets through the streets, Yelda put them into a secret pocket she had sewn into her school bag. Sometimes she even glued it shut. She hoped if she were searched by police, they would not find the papers.

The leaflets told the truth about what the Soviets were doing and urged young people to resist the occupation. Since all news was controlled, it was important for people to find out about the resistance. Yelda and her two RAWA friends divided their high school into three sections for distributing secret leaflets: the first floor, the second floor, and the schoolyard. Yelda took the first floor. She waited until everyone was outside for recess. Then she dashed into an empty classroom, or even the principal's office, and left a leaflet. Since so many of the students were against the Soviets, when someone found one, she would pass it on.

In April 1980, the Karmal regime announced it would hold celebrations of the second anniversary of their "Revolution." When the Soviets had invaded, they had promised their occupation was temporary, but they refused to leave. People who opposed Karmal and the Soviets planned a huge protest. Not only RAWA, but many other groups passed the word. As it turned out, the leaflet for that demonstration was the last one Yelda helped to distribute at her high school, because it caused her to go into hiding.

The mobilization started near Kabul University, and spread from high school to high school until tens of thousands of students were in the streets, trying to march to government buildings to voice their demands. They asked for Soviet withdrawal and the resignation of the politicians who had invited them into the country. Yelda decided to go. The slogans on the signs the protestors held said: NO COMMUNIST REGIME. USSR OUT. DEMOCRACY NOW.

When the students were met by pro-Soviet Afghan soldiers, some girls took off their head scarves and threw them at the heads of the men, taunting them to put them on and calling them "Soviet slaves" and "women"—unfortunately, a sexist insult to Afghan men. Yelda did not think "woman" was an insult, so she called the soldiers "traitors."

Yelda was overjoyed when she saw every one of her fellow students at the high school walk out of their classes and gather in the courtyard, ready to march out. But then the principal got a phone call from the police ordering her to close the gates. The gatekeeper locked the girls in, but they pushed him aside and broke the lock with stones. By the time they got the gates open, the street outside was already filled with dozens of policemen, armed with tear gas and electric cattle prods. Among them were agents of the Soviet-Afghan secret police, the KHAD, who were making notes on anyone they thought was a leader so that later they could arrest them, or even kill them.

The leaflets announcing the demonstration had called for non-violence. Even though the students did not attack the police, the police attacked them. Policemen forced their way into the schoolyard, tear-gassed the students, and beat them. Yelda was stung on her thigh by a cattle prod. Her whole leg was numb.

By evening, the news spread throughout Kabul that two girls had been killed by the police. One was a girl named Naheed, from Amina Fadawi High School, who had climbed up on a Soviet tank. Soldiers had taken aim and shot her dead. The other girl, Wadjia, from Rabia Balkhi High School, was picked out as a ringleader and also killed. Both were seventeen years old. Many people had been arrested; but the next day, thousands demonstrated again, to protest the killing of the two girls. The third day, so many students were arrested and beaten that finally the demonstrations subsided.

Many of those taken into custody were never seen again. The RAWA girls found out that the principal had put Yelda's name on a list of troublemakers. Known as an activist, she couldn't go back to school. Yelda's RAWA friends helped her to go into hiding in Kabul. They invited her to leave for Pakistan to work with the organization there. But Yelda was too afraid to be so far from her family. She still met secretly with RAWA, but was no longer able to move around the city.

Sadaf was still teaching and secretly helping her students to take part in the resistance. During the big demonstrations, one of Sadaf's students was arrested with a leaflet in her possession. Under questioning, she gave in and told the police that Sadaf was the one who had given it to her.

Immediately, Sadaf was arrested. She had been on maternity leave, caring for her firstborn child, a daughter only forty days old. She would not leave her baby, so she took her to prison with her.

Sadaf's husband also opposed the regime. When she was arrested, he made the wrenching decision to leave Kabul, certain that he would soon be taken away, too. He escaped to Pakistan.

The police threw Sadaf and her baby into a cell with seventy other women. There were a number of other babies.

The cell was far too small for so many people. There was only one toilet to share, very little food, and only the floor to sleep on. Sadaf and her baby lived in that cell for two and a half years without a trial or access to legal representation. During that time, some women were released, but new prisoners came in all the time. Some died from lack of medical care. Sadaf had nothing but her own strength and the support of three other RAWA members in the cell to sustain her. Two of her cellmates were also founding members of RAWA.

Living with her baby in that cell, Sadaf thought of Meena and her daughter. Now that she was a mother, she realized what a heroic sacrifice it had been for Meena to give up her baby. Even when she was arrested, Sadaf couldn't bear to be separated from her child. The baby grew, and learned to walk and talk, knowing nothing but the inside of a prison.

It was a bitter blow to Sadaf that several of her prison guards were women who had been her students at Malalai High School. Some guards knew Meena because they had been at school together. Meena was also known to the guards because the police were searching for her. Sadaf's guards tried to torment her by telling her that Meena had fled to Europe to lead a life of luxury. They would taunt her, "You're a teacher, you should not have listened to one of your students."

Because of Meena's husband, the guards tried to accuse the RAWA prisoners of being Maoists. They resisted this label. "One thing RAWA has never hidden is our politics," Sadaf told an officer. "If I were some kind of Soviet or Chinese communist, I would not deny it, but I'm not. I know you can't imagine that a woman can have her own politics, different from her husband's. Yet in Meena's case, it's the truth."

Another RAWA prisoner added, "The world over, women are painted with their husbands' opinions. Afghan women are far, far away from even basic knowledge and respect, let alone freedom and equality. Why should we want either the Soviet way or the Chinese way, when they don't offer us these things?"

In the Afghan countryside, armed resistance to the Soviets began in 1980. That summer, the United States boycotted the Olympics, which were held in Moscow, to protest the U.S.S.R.'s invasion of Afghanistan.

Afghan men formed guerrilla armies of *mujahedeen*—holy warriors—which mobilized under local commanders. The mujahedeen fought, not only to rid the nation of invaders, but to defend Islam against Russians they regarded as infidels. In fierce fighting in the countryside, they forced the withdrawal of *Khalq*, *Parcham*, and Soviet troops from most rural areas. In response, the Soviets and the puppet Afghan army bombed villages with explosives and napalm, and scattered land mines in fields and along roads in an attempt to rout the fighters. Men, women, and children were maimed and killed in dozens of villages over a period of years.

There was no central leadership or national army fighting the war on the Afghan side because the diverse tribes were unable to unify. That greatly hampered their war effort.

Individual *mujahedeen* commanders fought in each area, each with his own men. When they won territory from the Soviets, they set up personal fiefdoms. The *mujahedeen* were more skilled at fighting than governing. Some of them set themselves up as fundamentalist dictators. Their soldiers were mostly poorly trained, illiterate young men, who destroyed schools and clinics, killed teachers and doctors, stole from peasants and raped women. The fundamentalist *mujahedeen* enforced a cruel version of *Sharia* law that excused whatever crimes their soldiers had committed and punished anyone who questioned their rule. Villagers and nomads were often caught between the Soviet tanks and guns and the crimes of the fundamentalist *mujahedeen* soldiers and commanders.

Some of the Afghan fighters upheld the democratic values that were being threatened by both the Soviets and the fundamentalist *mujahedeen*. These democratic *mujahedeen* fought bravely and tried to contribute to freeing their country from the Soviets without allying themselves with the fundamentalists.

Both sides of the war forced young men into their armies. The *Khalq* government conscripted boys to be sent to the front to fight on the side of the Soviets. Any family that resisted was subject to arrest. There was a tradition in Afghanistan that if a family had only one male, he was excused from military service because he was the only provider. The Soviets not only abolished that law, they imposed military terms that varied according to educational status: College graduates were conscripted for two years and high school graduates for three years. Young men without schooling had to serve four years.

RAWA responded with leaflets warning people about the conscription and urging public demonstrations against the government. RAWA printed and distributed an article about how mothers were resisting sending their sons into the *Khalq*/Soviet army. The article told a story of one mother who begged the soldiers not to take her only son. He was given only a month of training and then sent directly into combat. After one month of fighting, he was killed.

Even though they were working for women's rights, after the Soviet invasion, the most important thing to the democratic forces like RAWA was to join the fight against Soviet occupation. RAWA supported the Afghan war of resistance and provided as much support for the democratic *mujahedeen* as possible. RAWA developed strong contacts with doctors and nurses, and helped to send mobile medical teams into the provinces to help wounded civilians and guerrilla fighters. The Soviets controlled the roads to the cities, making access to hospitals impossible. RAWA's rural contacts were invaluable to medical workers trying to aid the resistance.

But throughout the war, Meena insisted on telling the truth about both sides. Meena and the other RAWA leaders were faced with negotiating a narrow political path between the Soviets and the *mujahedeen*. In a test of their principles, they developed a sophisticated critique of both, in an atmosphere in which the entire nation was being forced to choose sides between two deadly alternatives. Meena refused to turn a blind eye to the mistakes and crimes of the fundamentalist *mujahedeen*. From the beginning, she upheld the principle of absolute honesty. She made sure that RAWA's leaflets condemned the outrages of the fundamentalists against the people. RAWA never hesitated openly to criticize anyone with blood on their hands. No matter how desperate the struggle, RAWA never allied with fundamentalist *mujahedeen* in order to fight the Soviets.

Meena personally visited women who had family members in prison, and made them feel less alone. Through her, they felt they were among thousands of others living with the same pain and grief.

Meena heard about a desperate family of Tajik women living alone in Kabul. The father, brothers, uncles, and male cousins had all been taken away and executed in 1978—not for being in any political party, but just for being educated people. Even though there were thousands of such families, Meena felt that she had to begin somewhere. Without even an introduction, she went to visit them, asking if there was any way she could be of help. The women were amazed that Meena, a stranger and a Pashtun, would visit them, a Tajik family. Basera, the oldest daughter, was petite and soft-spoken, with finely chiseled features and lovely eyes that showed her Tajik heritage. She was a senior science student at Lycée Malalai. She had taken part in the 1979 and 1980 student strikes, but was not a RAWA member.

Once or twice a week, Meena arrived at Basera's house wearing her old *burqa* and shoes. To have an excuse to be out walking, she usually carried water buckets. At first, Basera and her mother were sure Meena was a spy. They acted friendly to her, but didn't tell her anything. Though they could not fully trust her, they began to look forward to her visits.

The older women, Basera's mother and grandmother, were especially depressed and fragile. Once, when Meena arrived, the television was on, showing a Russian detective program that depicted torture and murder. Basera's grandmother and mother were so upset by it that they were crying.

Basera said, "I can't believe they are not ashamed to show what they do." Meena strode over, turned the set off, and went to make tea. She sat down and talked with Basera's grandmother and mother to take their minds off their troubles. Basera could feel Meena bringing life back into their home and opening its walls to the outside world.

When Meena and Basera first met, Basera was severely depressed. She bore a burden of guilt that weighed on her. She had given a leaflet to one of her male cousins who was a student at the Polytechnic High School, and he showed it to someone who had informed. He disappeared and was never seen again. No one could find out what had happened to him. Meena told Basera, "Your cousin's death was not your fault. It was the fault of this murderous regime."

Finally, after five months of making friends, Meena felt she knew Basera and her family well enough to trust them. She told all of them about RAWA. "Even though the whole society undervalues what women can do, we have a lot to contribute, both in the fight against the Soviets and against women's conditions."

Meena asked Basera and all three of her sisters to join RAWA.

Basera and her sisters all made the decision to join, not just because their father and brothers and uncles had been killed, but because they saw that Meena was someone who cared. RAWA gave them a reason to hope.

At first, Basera and her sisters had no particular duties as RAWA members. Meena visited them, and, like a teacher, she would talk to them about RAWA's ideals and give them RAWA's reports on what was happening. The girls were all students, and Meena encouraged them to stay in school, help younger students to study, and try to raise their consciousness about the resistance.

The Soviets were recruiting in the high schools. They urged children to spy on their own families and turn them in. Students were exhorted to tell the teachers if their parents prayed at home. To students who showed enthusiasm for the indoctrination programs, they offered scholarships to Soviet-bloc countries.

On one occasion, Meena arrived at Basera's house exhausted. She had just arrived back in Kabul, having come from Pakistan. Nevertheless, she led a lively discussion for Basera and her sisters. They gathered around her to listen and ask her questions.

Meena told them, "In the name of workers' power, the Soviets enslave workers. RAWA is founded on freedom and equality for women and rights for everyone," she said.

"How will we ever make progress when so many Afghan women are afraid to try to change anything about their lives?" Basera asked.

"Afghan women are like sleeping lions," Meena said. "When we are aroused, we react with the same courage and charisma as lions. There are only two paths to choose from: Side with the criminal regime, or oppose them, and be ready to fight like lionesses. We might have to risk our lives, and even lose them."

Meena had brought books for the sisters to read. She gave them *The Mother* by Maxim Gorky, and *Jamila* by Aitmatov, both of them feminist stories of women's suffering that were available in

Kabul because they were written by Russian male authors. Meena also gave Basera and her sisters a RAWA pamphlet, written anonymously by members, titled "I Vow I'll Go the Way You're Going." It was the true story of a girl whose brother had volunteered to fight against the Soviets, and had been killed. When the girl saw his body, she vowed to follow in his footsteps and join the resistance movement.

By 1981, so many people had been arrested and disappeared in the wake of the demonstrations that holding more public protests seemed impossible. The people were afraid and discouraged. With the press censored, they had no way of knowing what was happening. Meena conceived a bold idea. She formed a committee of RAWA women to work on putting out a publication that would encourage women to participate in the struggle against the Soviets.

RAWA decided to produce a small magazine, which they named *Payam-e-Zan—Women's Message*. Paper was scarce, and very expensive. They had no access to a printing press. They typed out several pages of text and hand-pasted the pictures. Meena wrote several of the articles herself. Secretly making copies on an old mimeograph machine, they managed to produce a first issue of about a thousand copies in April 1981. They were ready in time for the anniversary of the deaths of the girls in the big demonstrations of the year before.

Payam-e-Zan documented the abuses and violence of the regime. But more important for women, *Payam-e-Zan* was the only publication in the country about women, documenting the threats to them and their resistance.

The first issue had a dimly reproduced photo on the front cover of the round-faced high school girl Naheed, who had been shot down in the April 1980 mass uprising. The accompanying article said: "She sacrificed her life for the people. She became a star in heaven and will live in our memories forever. She had just been married, and her hands still had henna painted on them."

The first issue also contained an unsigned poem by Meena written in the passionate and flowery Farsi style of verse:

I Shall Never Turn Back
by Meena

I'm the woman who has awakened
I've risen and become a tempest through the ashes of
   my burnt children
I've risen from the rivulets of my brother's blood
My nation's wrath has empowered me
My ruined and burnt villages fill me with hatred
   against the enemy,
No longer think of me as weak and incapable, O
   Compatriot
I'm the woman who has awakened,
I've found my path and will never turn back.

Those shackles on my feet I have broken
I've opened the closed doors of ignorance
I've said farewell to all golden bracelets
O Compatriot, O brother of mine, I'm not what I
   was
I'm the woman who has awakened
I've found my path and will never turn back.

With my penetrating insight, I have seen everything
   in the pitch-darkness enveloping my country,
The midnight screams of bereaved mothers still reso-
   nate in my ears
I've seen barefoot, wandering and homeless children
I've seen henna-handed brides with mourning clothes
I've seen giant walls of the prisons swallow freedom
   in their ravenous stomach
I've been reborn amidst epics of resistance and
   courage
I've learned the song of freedom in the last breaths,
   in the waves of blood and in victory

O Compatriot, O brother, no longer regard me as
  weak and incapable
With all my strength I'm with you on the path of my
  land's liberation.
My voice has mingled with thousands of arisen
  women
My fists are clenched with the fists of thousands of
  compatriots
Along with you I've stepped up to the path of my
  nation,
To break all this suffering, all these fetters of
  slavery,
O Compatriot, O brother, I'm not what I was
I'm the woman who has awakened
I've found my path and will never turn back.

The women risked their lives to deliver *Payam-e-Zan* to members and supporters. They were passed from hand to hand among trusted friends and neighbors. *Payam-e-Zan* became the preferred reading material for RAWA's literacy classes.

The Soviets had imposed a curfew in Kabul that kept people indoors after dark and before dawn, making movement from one place to another even more difficult.

Roya, who was so skilled at smuggling messages into the prison, excelled at distributing *Payam-e-Zan*. Roya could not read it herself, but she wanted its precious pages of news and poems to reach as many women as possible, and she risked her life to make it happen. She asked another RAWA member to read it aloud to her.

Meena and Roya worked as partners. They had to cross checkpoints all over the city. It was terrifying to approach the bands of soldiers holding automatic rifles, stand in line, and try to avoid being searched. Meena insisted on being the one to carry the magazines. She packed a pile of *Payam-e-Zan* in her bag underneath sewing cloth and a lot of beautiful thread, and then she placed a box of chocolates on top. When once a soldier searched Meena's bag, Roya stood watching, holding her breath. He stopped searching when he saw the chocolate. He took it for himself and let them go.

The two smugglers had a lot of these close calls. Once, they were trying to take magazines into the De Afphonen neighborhood in Kabul, but saw the police had surrounded the house where they were headed. Worried for their friends, they had no choice but to turn away and take the copies back through the checkpoints with them.

Meena never wanted to endanger Roya. She wouldn't let Roya go inside the homes with her, in case the police were inside or the house was raided while she was in there. She told Roya, "Wait for me. If I don't come back in ten minutes, leave immediately."

Articles in the next issue of *Payam-e-Zan*, dated July 1981, described the risks students took in the face of repression:

> Students from Zaherguna High were very clever. They had a meeting in the schoolyard and planned their demonstration. The first thing they did was cut the school's phone lines. Therefore, the authorities could not bring the police forces to arrest them or kill them. Then they took to the streets and joined other students.

> A girl named Fahima from Arenah High School was shot by the U.S.S.R. soldiers near the Kabul River. Her body was pushed and pulled like a dead animal, still bleeding, her clothes coming off. A male student from Anghlab School tried to rescue her, but he was also shot and killed. People who witnessed it say they can still hear their cries for help. Soon the U.S.S.R. soldiers took over the streets with tanks, and immediately the iron gates of all the schools were closed, trapping the students inside until long after the normal time to go home. Once the streets were secured by the Soviet army, the students were slowly released in small groups. The next day the schools were closed in most parts of Kabul.

This was the kind of information the Soviets went to great lengths to suppress. Their hunt for the publishers of *Payam-e-Zan* was intense. The police came to Meena's parents' house, searched it, and questioned everyone. Where was she? How did they get news of her? No one told them anything. One of her little brothers, not even a teenager yet, was taken to jail, beaten, then released when he said nothing.

Though Meena's activities frightened her family, they tried to support her. One evening, Meena's favorite uncle heard a pebble hit the window of his house. He and his wife went to the door and an agitated Meena slipped inside. She stayed only a few minutes, long enough to kiss them and to tell them to burn their photos of her. Reluctantly, they did so.

One of RAWA's supporters got a warning that her home was probably going to be searched. She got a message to Meena. RAWA had been storing books for the literacy classes in the woman's house, which had to be moved to safety immediately.

"I can't afford to lose even *one* of these precious books," Meena said to Roya. "Please help me find somewhere to hide them."

Roya suggested the house of a farmer she knew outside of the city. They packed the books into four bundles, and waited for night, after curfew. Dressed in dark clothes, and each carrying two heavy bags, they walked anxiously for miles through the fields in the dark. The wheat had been harvested already, so there was no place to hide. On their way back, soldiers in tanks were out patrolling the fields, and there was no cover. When lights were shone on them, they threw themselves onto the ground. When they got back, Meena was covered with cuts and bruises.

Though Meena was physically fragile, she could never fully repress the mischievous side of her personality. To Roya's horror, a few times she dressed in trousers and a man's jacket, and with her hair pushed up under a man's cap, she went out in the dim light of evening and rode a bicycle through Kabul's back streets.

"How can you endanger yourself so recklessly?" Roya asked her.

"I'm sick of being blinded and hobbled by the *burqa*," Meena said. "And besides, I always carry pepper. If a police patrol stops me, my plan is to throw it into their eyes and try to run."

Roya thought this plan was unrealistic, but she could only shake her head at Meena's irrepressible daring.

While RAWA was building up its networks in Afghanistan, in Pakistan, Gulbaddin Hekmatyar's fundamentalist *Hezb-e-Islami* party was building its networks, too. With support from the Pakistani government and secret police, they set up hundreds of religious schools for boys—*madrassas*—along the border area. In the areas controlled by the fundamentalists, girls were prohibited from attending any school. Pakistan's school system was in a state of collapse, so the *madrassas* were the only chance poor Pakistani and Afghan refugee boys had for some semblance of an education. Instruction consisted of rote recitation of the Koran in Arabic, and brainwashing in the narrow, *Sharia* code of antiwomen laws. In 1971, there were only 900 *madrassas* in Pakistan, but by 1980, there were over 10,000, with over 250,000 students, funded by the Islamic governments of several nations, especially Saudi Arabia. Hekmatyar's party received the lion's share of this aid.

One wealthy Saudi family that supported the fundamentalist movement with funds was the large bin Laden clan. Osama bin Laden had been born in 1957, the same year as Meena's birth. In 1980, he visited the *mujahedeen* leaders in Pakistan, bringing millions of dollars in donations for their cause. He and Meena were both twenty-three years old.

10

EUROPE

The second issue of RAWA's newsletter *Payam-e-Zan* featured this brief article:

> A RAWA member named Faridah Ahmady and her sister were arrested and jailed for five months. They were both tortured by agents of the KHAD—the secret police—while in custody. After they were freed, RAWA helped them to get to Pakistan. The International Red Cross sent them to a hospital in France to be treated for their wounds and for mental trauma. Once they had recovered, they traveled to England, Norway, Switzerland, and the United States, speaking about the plight of women in Afghanistan. They did not return, but were granted refugee status in Norway, where they continue to work for Afghan women.

RAWA was beginning to attract the attention of a few people abroad. Human rights organizations wrote reports and issued condemnations, but most people the world over ignored what was happening to Afghans.

In France, the 1981 elections brought the new socialist government of François Mitterand to power. The Afghan *Khalq* government also called itself "socialist," but the French leaders parted ways with the Soviets over Afghanistan. Through supporters in France, the Mitterand government began a relationship with RAWA instead. Soon, a letter came to Pakistan, asking RAWA to send a representative to France to attend the International Socialist Conference. The French Socialist Party offered to pay expenses for a delegate to come to Europe.

Everyone in RAWA wanted Meena to go, and she agreed. But she had no passport, and it was impossible to obtain one from the Afghan puppet government. RAWA members in Pakistan set about doing what was necessary to obtain a forged passport. Meena's family name could not be revealed, for the sake of her relatives' safety. RAWA chose a false surname that sounded Indian, not Afghan— "Keshwar Kamel." An Indian name would allow Meena to more easily pass through India, the easiest route from Afghanistan to Europe.

The hardest part of the journey was the beginning. From Kabul, Meena had to travel over the dangerous road to the Pakistan border, heavily patrolled by police and soldiers. Battles frequently broke out when the *mujahedeen*, hiding in the surrounding mountains, attacked the soldiers. Civilians passing through this guerrilla war were sometimes wounded or killed in the cross fire. The road had been bombed and shelled so many times, no asphalt was left on it. Cars, buses, and trucks had to navigate seas of mud, dust, or ice chewed into deep ruts by the metal treads of tanks. Both sides of the road were heavily mined with explosives powerful enough to blow up a meandering car or bus. A misstep could kill or maim, and often did.

Setting off in her *burqa*, Meena boarded a crowded bus, hoping to pass as a member of a group going to visit relatives. The road, an ancient trade route, leaves Kabul's high plateau and drops through steep mountain canyons alongside raging river torrents. It emerges from the mountains into a series of fertile valleys, with views of snowy peaks on all sides. Lower down, there are orchards and emerald green rice paddies, and lower still, mud-walled villages surrounded by date palm trees. Nomadic peoples pitch their tents along the road and graze their camels nearby.

Meena's bus began to climb again and finally reached the Khyber Pass, a low place in the dry desert mountains that lie between Afghanistan and Pakistan.

Gazing out the window, Meena longed for peace for her beloved country. She had written a poem which expressed her feelings for Afghanistan, which she called "The Great Love."

The Great Love

I love my country with a great love

because even its towering mountains
have risen to stand against the intruders,

because even its rivers are raging more fiercely than
  ever before,
they break free of their banks
to flood and wash out the roads the invaders would
  travel,
and because of its people I love my country,

my people who will never bow down or obey
even after their villages have fallen in ruins,

my people who rise up to join in protest
even after their cities run red with blood and fire.

I love my country with a great love

because its daughters have exchanged their pens for
  daggers
and made of the chadors the black flags of freedom,
because its children, when they cry, are crying for
  freedom.

I love my country with a great love,

my tumultuous country,
which, in the middle of Asia, searches for peace
    alone,
it is drowning in innocent blood,
it is losing all hope of reaching the peaceful shore.

My country resists the invaders who bring their own
    ruin!
My country is tired of injustice and will swallow no
    more!
My country will never surrender to occupation!

I love my country with a great love, I hail this love
    and each of its lovers!

—Jane Hirschfield translation

Just before Meena's bus reached the border crossing, it stopped and most passengers got off, Meena among them. Few refugees had the necessary documents—passports, visas, or customs declarations—to pass through the high metal gates at the Khyber Pass that mark the official border. Most left the road on foot at the border and set off over the mountains. Meena, too, walked. She followed a narrow path worn by the feet of migrants and smugglers. It winds up from the Afghan side, climbing through the canyons and over the peaks. There are no villages in the border no-man's-land, no place to rest or buy food.

The two nations meet in an ill-defined border zone a thousand miles long and a hundred miles wide that runs along the desert edge of the Indian subcontinent—dry wastelands that have never been governed by anyone. Robbers, heroin traffickers, and weapons dealers thrive there, and smugglers cache their loot—drugs, weapons, and all sorts of goods from electronics to textiles—among the endless canyons and crags.

Each border region bears the name of one of the desert and

mountain peoples who live there: Waziristan, Kurram, Orakazai, Khyber, Mohmand, and Bajaur. Violence between tribes has long been as constant as smuggling. Government attempts to quell the fighting have been met with bomb blasts and gunfire. No Afghan or Pakistani regime has subdued these areas. No one collects taxes, arrests criminals, or rescues the injured.

Many travelers pay a guide to take them through the confusing maze of pathways. Walking in late summer, Meena risked heat stroke and thirst. Every woman traversing the Khyber Pass faced the always-present danger of rape or murder.

On the Pakistan side, there was the long descent down the trail to the road again. Exhausted, Meena boarded another bus for the last few hours' drive into the city of Peshawar, where her husband was waiting for her. It was one of their rare times together, and though they had to be careful, they spent precious hours alone. They talked about the sweet things their daughter was doing and saying, and the exciting journey to Europe ahead of Meena.

After a few days' rest, she crossed Pakistan, made a dangerous illegal crossing into India with her false documents, and boarded a plane for the first time in her life.

Meena landed first in Paris, a city that seemed like a dream from her student days at Malalai, where the French teachers had talked so much of home. Her first impression was of freedom. It was wonderful to be in a place without war, a place where she could walk freely in the streets without fear of arrest or attack. Once she realized she was safe, it was as if something loosened in her chest, and she could breathe more deeply. Everything seemed so clean, everyone so comfortable, and above all, so safe that people seemed to have a kind of innocence or naïveté.

Meena had no time to pause and take in her reactions. She immediately set out to do what she had come to do: to speak for her people. It seemed at first as if it would be impossible for her to convey to her French hosts where she had come from.

But Meena's natural poise came to her aid, and she spoke confidently, answering questions nonstop. She was amazed to learn that some people had no idea where Afghanistan was. And she was bemused by the many people who openly expressed surprise at her light skin; they had assumed that Afghans were Arabs with darker complexions.

The socialist world was powerful and expanding in 1982. Many nations (including Italy and Germany, as well as France) had socialist governments or large socialist or communist parties. Hundreds of delegates descended on the small French city of Valence for the International Socialist Conference in October 1981. An article on the front page of *Le Monde* noted that there were representatives from 250 nations. Misspelling her pseudonym, it mentions, "*la représentante de la résistance afghane*, Mme. Keshmar Kamel."

The conference hall was filled with tremendous tensions. The U.S.S.R. had sent a very high-level delegation, headed by Boris Ponomarev, who had been a member of the Central Committee of the Communist Party of the Soviet Union and chief of its International Department since 1955. It was Ponomarev who orchestrated Soviet influence over governments in Africa, the Middle East, and Asia, and he who oversaw the invasion of Afghanistan. No other man was more responsible for the devastation of the Afghan occupation.

The Chinese-Russian split within the communist world most captured the attention of the news media. The U.S.S.R.'s archenemies, the Chinese Communist Party, were also heavily represented in the hall. But the other confrontation to occur there was between tiny Afghanistan and the Soviet Empire.

When Meena rose to address the congress, she was one of a minority of women speakers there. Her daunting responsibility was to represent not just women, but all of Afghanistan's struggle for freedom. Many of the people at the conference represented countries so dominated by the U.S.S.R., they would never dare to openly criticize the superpower they depended upon. The general worldview of the socialist movement was that national liberation struggles were waged only against the colonialism of the Western powers, and never against a socialist state. What Meena had to say was absolute heresy in that setting.

The Soviet Union had provided crucial aid to the Vietnamese and their victory over the Americans. The Russians held themselves out as liberators; at the same time they were decimating Afghanistan in a war that nearly mirrored the U.S. war on Vietnam.

Meena did have allies in the conference hall: The French Socialist Party, critical of the invasion of Afghanistan, had invited her. Yet it required tremendous courage for anyone to stand up and ask the support of the socialist world for a liberation movement that was fighting against the U.S.S.R for its freedom. When Meena walked to the podium, she exposed her face to the Soviet secret police. She knew that from that moment, they would try to hunt her down and kill her.

It was an incongruous confrontation: the beautiful young woman, only twenty-four years old, head of a small but determined group of women, many of them widows and young girls, boldly facing Ponomarev, the crusty and dangerous older man who could order legions of tanks, airplanes, soldiers, and spies to do his bidding.

Meena spoke simply and from her own heart of the suffering of the women who were depending on her at home. She described how her nation had risen as one against the invaders, old and young, men and women. Meena told the world about the thousands who had been imprisoned, and the thousands executed. She held nothing back. She exposed in graphic terms the torture inflicted by the Soviets and their puppets. "They do not hesitate to apply electric shocks to the ears, tongues, or genitals of their victims. They rip out fingernails and toenails. If a woman does not confess, they bring in her husband to watch her being raped.

"Even kindergartens refuse to accept donations of milk from them. Men as old as seventy are fighting with our men at the front. Resistance has ceased to be a matter of age or gender." Meena vowed that Afghans would never stop fighting until the Soviet Union was expelled from Afghanistan.

When she finished, the delegates rose to their feet to give her a prolonged standing ovation, as she stood smiling and waving from the podium. Boris Ponomarev and his delegation got up, turned their backs, and stalked out of the hall.

Meena remained in France for some weeks, meeting with officials and supporters. She had long talks with French Prime Minister Pierre Mauroy and with the General Secretary of the French Socialist Party. In West Germany, she met with the Foreign Minister's staff, and in Belgium, she gave public talks in Brussels and The Hague. She also spoke in Norway.

A photo of Meena appeared in the Hamburg, Germany, newspaper *Hamburger Abendblatt*, on January 19, 1982. The accompanying article said, "She travelled by bus and on foot on little paths, disguised by traditional tribal dress."

The German reporter described Meena: "Her way of speaking is assertive yet always thoughtful, which reminds one of the young Golda Meir . . . Her black eyes sparkle, the eyes of the woman who, since 1980, has actively been leading the underground Afghan women's resistance against the Soviets and their puppet regime in Kabul."

The article quoted Meena: "Babrak Karmal and his people would not last a single hour if the Russians were to withdraw their troops. An area seventeen kilometers around Kabul is ruled by the Soviets and Karmal's troops. Everything else, apart from Soviet bases and the other cities they hold, is ruled by resistance fighters."

Asked about repression against RAWA, Meena said, "During the last two years of terror and suppression, we have lost a great number of our members. They were tortured, and many were executed." She told of a woman she knew well, who, seven months pregnant, was arrested and first whipped and then beaten with wooden clubs to extract information about RAWA's resistance.

"We women carry our resistance leaflets under our *burqa*; of course, the Russians know about that," she said with a little smile, "but how can they possibly check every single veiled woman?"

Asked how they protect themselves against spies, Meena replied,

Meena speaking at a
press conference.

Meena triumphantly waves the sign for "Victory" to the delegates at
the Congress of the French Socialist Party in France, 1981.

A still photo from
the film clip of
Meena speaking
in Brussels.

"We meticulously check on each new member. At first a new woman will just do errands, such as carrying messages. Only much later will she be told about the structure of our organization."

Asked about the future of women in Afghanistan, she said that the struggle to liberate the nation would also provide "a big chance to further women's equality in our country. There won't be a patriarchal system as there was before the occupation of Afghanistan."

A five-minute fragment of a 1981 interview Meena gave to a Brussels television station has survived. Meena's flickering image appears on a damaged, aging piece of videotape, a copy of a copy.

Her hair is uncovered, and styled in a short European cut, curling around her face. One can imagine her—maybe with a new French friend—visiting a salon in Paris and having it styled. She is dressed in a blue turtleneck shirt under a blue-and-white-patterned wool sweater. What everyone who met her has said is true: She is uncommonly lovely. Off camera, a man's voice questions her in French.

Meena's black eyes reveal so much, the viewer can literally see her quick mind working as she considers the question, as if she is thinking about the issue on many levels, the big picture and the details. Then she speaks, with assurance and poise, of the Soviets' use of toxic gas, of the gunfire that is heard every day in Afghan cities. She gestures with a pen she holds in her right hand.

Through a female translator, Meena says: "Though currently there is no proper national front, more than 99 percent of the Afghan people are battling in scattered contingents against the Russians. . . . However, there are some elements in the country that owing to political interests, seek to create cracks in this national movement. These Afghan fanatics are now present in Peshawar, and are willing to have a Khomeini type of regime [an Islamist extremist regime like the one that had taken over in Iran] for the country."

A modern-day Cassandra, Meena was trying to warn the world. In the Greek myth, Cassandra foretold the gory defeat of Troy, but no one would believe her.

Only a few weeks before the tape of Meena was made, Egypt had become the first state to suffer the consequences of the arming of the fundamentalist *mujahedeen* fighters by the U.S. and the Saudi Arabian royal family. Egyptian Muslim extremists, trained in camps in Pakistan, returned to Egypt and assassinated President Anwar Sadat on October 6, 1981. Sadat had drawn the wrath of the fanatics when he signed a peace treaty with Israel. Egyptian extremists later attacked women, Christians, Western tourists, and every subsequent Egyptian government.

Only a tiny handful of people realized the danger the extremists posed to the world. Meena was trying her best to be heard, but few would listen to an Afghan woman.

As she speaks on the video, Meena's charisma journeys across the lost years. It is easy to see why so many who met her wanted to stay near her and follow her. There is an unmistakable combination of softness and strength.

As her tour progressed, letters from the RAWA leaders in Pakistan begged Meena to stay in Europe. They knew her life was in danger. She refused. She wrote to Asifa, "I have to return to breathe the air of Afghanistan—at least to be close to it in Pakistan. I can only be effective if I come home."

Meena returned to Pakistan on June 2, 1982, after a journey of eight months. She was given a heroine's welcome by her husband and the RAWA women, all of them delighted by her success. Later, she told Mowaish, laughing, "Faiz teased me. He said he thinks the delegates at the conference gave me a standing ovation not only because I was eloquent, but also because I'm beautiful."

Meena immediately began work on getting out another, the fourth, issue of *Payam-e-Zan*. In the 1982 issue, a short article, published anonymously but in Meena's unmistakable style, said: "In a very short time, the women of Afghanistan have achieved the ability to stand up against the enemy. Because of their resistance, RAWA was invited to represent Afghanistan in a conference in Valence, France, on October 22, 1981. A member addressed the representatives on the opening day and described the political situation of women in Afghanistan and their daily struggle against the occupation. She told about how women are jailed and tortured because of fighting the occupiers, how innocents are bombed and peaceful demonstrators are jailed, including women and young girls, how women are left without husbands, whose lives were taken by the barbaric government forced on them by the Soviets."

The issue also had a report of the visit to Pakistan that year by two Norwegian women journalists who came to research the situation of women and children in the refugee camps. "They met with women, many of them villagers from different parts of Afghanistan. They saw the active role of women directly and indirectly impacting the war against the U.S.S.R. They also expressed their interest in helping Afghan people by writing about them and voicing their concerns."

But most of the world remained blind to what was going on inside Afghanistan.

Now that her face was known to the highest Soviet officials, Kabul was even more dangerous for Meena, but she returned there in the late summer of 1982. She longed to see her daughter, who was about to turn three years old. Meena had not seen her for nearly a year, their longest separation.

The authorities had publicly called for Meena's arrest. They had circulated pictures of Meena to the soldiers guarding the checkpoints on the main roads. Spies were everywhere. The Soviet KGB had built up an enormous Afghan intelligence force, the KHAD, which had at least fifteen thousand employees, and one hundred thousand paid informants. People were so desperate for the means to survive that the money offered by the KHAD was tempting. Even fundamentalists often changed sides temporarily to work as spies or gunmen for the occupiers.

In spite of the dangers, Meena insisted on leaving the relative safety of Pakistan to return to Afghanistan, to lead and support the women whose organization straddled two countries. When those who loved her told her they were worried for her, she often replied, "Women should take the same risks men are taking."

Roya was one of Meena's most trusted companions. The tough village woman was resourceful in a way Meena could rely on. Both of them were intrepid, and together they made a great team. Two good friends, invisible in plain sight, traipsed about Kabul under the noses of the police, going where they needed to go.

While Roya's husband was in prison—he was held for two years and seven months—Roya lived with his parents, who were conservative people. They could not be told what Roya was doing. She had told them Meena was her cousin, so that she could get out of the house to meet her.

Roya sneaked out one September day in 1982 and met Meena and two other RAWA women for a special mission. They crossed Kabul, carrying guns to the resistance fighters. They couldn't use taxis because they were searched too often. They took a bus, with the guns in bags, under their *burqas*. They boarded separately, at different stops, and made no contact on the bus. Meena told them, "When I squeeze my eyes at you, get off." They delivered the guns safely. Soon after, Meena left Kabul again, heading back to Pakistan to check on the refugee work there.

11

EXILE

One night, back in Kabul again, Meena violated her own rules. RAWA members avoided taxis, because they were so often stopped by the police. But pressed for time on the way to a meeting, five of them crowded in, Meena in back with two other RAWA women, all of them wearing *burqas*, two male supporters in the front seat with the driver. As the car approached an unexpected checkpoint, everyone hoped the police would wave them through, but the car was stopped.

Meena recognized one of the armed guards, a woman she had known at school. The policewoman leaned into the car window, shined her flashlight into the back seat, and demanded that the women lift their *burqas* and show their faces. One by one they did so. Meena was the last in line. She knew the policewoman would know her face. When she lifted her veil she'd be arrested.

At that moment, another car drove up, and the policewoman waved the taxi on. After this close call, the other RAWA leaders demanded that Meena leave Afghanistan immediately. Meena argued that she had too much work to do to leave, but they insisted. She had reached the end of her time to live and work in Kabul safely.

Where to go? Iran was not an option. Early in the Soviet occupation, some RAWA members had escaped to Iran, where eventually over a million Afghans took shelter. But Iran's Khomeini regime was so conservative that a feminist organization like RAWA

had no hope of operating there. RAWA had shifted all of its exile activities to Pakistan. Though the Pakistani government was also very conservative, it had far less control, especially over Afghan refugees.

Reluctantly, Meena packed to go. Exile for her, as for all refugees, was a defeat. The last thing she wanted to do was to leave the place of her birth, her only and beloved home. Her heart, and RAWA's, were in Afghanistan. Like refugees the world over, Meena left everything behind, packing only a small bundle she could carry. She chose a few precious things, some letters, a photo of her baby.

When the curfew lifted at 4:30 A.M., on an October morning in 1982, Asifa and Meena set out together. They went first to Mowaish's house to say good-bye. Meena wanted to see her daughter once more before leaving again, certainly for a long time, perhaps forever. On the way, slipping through the dawn with Asifa, she went over the decision she had made: "Unless there is a real danger to her in Kabul, I'm not going to take the baby with me," she told Asifa. "She's safer here, with Mowaish."

Several members of RAWA had spent the night at Mowaish's, and they were sleepily getting up. "Meena *jan*," the women whispered, kissing her—"Meena dear." Meena kissed each one and gave them notes she had written—last-minute instructions and personal remembrances. Some of them had tiny gifts for her—a handkerchief, a cassette of songs she loved.

Only Asifa knew that Mowaish's three-year-old little girl was Meena's daughter. Asifa, Mowaish, and Meena tiptoed into the room where the tiny girl lay warm and deep asleep, unaware that her mother had come. Meena bent down and kissed her. Then she silently began to cry.

Asifa took her into her arms and Meena whispered, crying, "I feel so guilty for bringing her into this world, because of what I must do." All three of them—mother, foster mother, and friend—silently shed tears together as the baby slept.

As Meena and Asifa left, the other women all wept to see them go. Meena never wanted to frighten or discourage anyone. Trying to hide her feelings, she pulled the *burqa* over her face. As terrible as it was for her to leave her little daughter, it was also hard to be forced to leave Afghanistan, not knowing if she would ever return.

She had to trust her fate, and RAWA's, to Pakistan, a nation only thirty-five years old and as destitute and in search of stability as the women were themselves.

Pakistan had been created out of turmoil and interreligious hatred in 1947. As the British left India, their former colony, they partitioned it into two nations, India and Pakistan. For centuries before that, Muslims and Hindus had lived intertwined. Two great leaders had opposed the division of India. Mahatma Gandhi was the Hindu leader of the nonviolent independence movement. Badshah Khan, a Pashtun, was Gandhi's Muslim counterpart. Together, they aroused Hindus and Muslims to struggle through nonviolent resistance to gain independence from the British. At the same time they appealed to the people of the two great and ancient religions to continue to live side by side and share their nation in peace.

There are many photos of the two leaders together—Badshah Khan, an imposing, handsome man nearly seven feet tall, towering over his diminutive partner and friend. In the end, Gandhi and Badshah Khan won their fight for freedom from the British, but lost the struggle for one nation. Pakistan was carved out of India in two sections hundreds of miles apart: West Pakistan was created next to Afghanistan. East Pakistan was adjacent to Burma. At the midnight hour of the new year in 1947, the new nations were born. Immediately, one of the most painful migrations in human history began. Millions of people left their homes, and many thousands died in violent clashes as the two peoples, who had once been one, pulled themselves apart.

In the 1970s, even more tragedy ensued as the two Pakistans warred. Finally, after thousands more died, they were severed into separate nations: Bangladesh in the east and Pakistan in the west.

By the time RAWA settled in Pakistan, the fate of nearly two million Afghan refugees depended on whoever ruled the country. Pakistan had been a Western-influenced modernizing nation when General Zia ul Haq took over in a coup in 1977. He turned the country sharply in a conservative Islamist direction, imposing both martial law and *Sharia* law. For RAWA, Pakistan's government was a frightening combination: a military dictatorship as well as an Islamic one.

As a balance to India on Pakistan's eastern border, Zia ul Haq was determined to help create an Islamic state in Afghanistan on his western border. The Afghan fundamentalist *mujahedeen* were perfect for his purposes. Zia armed these warlords with weapons supplied by the United States, and paid them with the Saudi petrodollars that poured into the country. Before the U.S./Saudi aid was over, it totaled over six billion dollars.

The money funded several warlord factions. Gulbaddin Hekmatyar's *Hezb-e-Islami* was the wealthiest and most powerful of them. Meena had feared and hated him since his days at the University of Kabul, where he had been involved in the murder of the young poet Saidal Sukhandan. RAWA had to watch as Hekmatyar and the others like him built fabulous villas for themselves and enlarged their private armies into formidable forces.

In 1982, Osama bin Laden moved to Pakistan. He settled in Peshawar, the stronghold of the fundamentalist warlords who dominated life in the otherwise lawless city. Bin Laden's family owned a huge construction firm. He brought engineers and heavy equipment with him to build roads and bases for the fundamentalist *mujahedeen*. He began work on the Khost tunnel complex in Afghanistan, deep under the mountains near the Pakistan border, which the CIA funded as a major arms depot for use against the Soviets.

Pakistan was far from a democracy. No matter who held the presidency, everyone knew that the real power lay in the hands of a sinister secret army, the Inter-Services Intelligence, called the I.S.I. This was the "invisible government" of Pakistan, implicated in assassinations and narcotics smuggling. United States foreign policy was so focused on defeating the Soviet Union that the CIA helped the I.S.I. with guns and money to train anti-Soviet Afghan fighters. With U.S. support, the I.S.I. grew stronger every year throughout the 1980s.

But the I.S.I. secret police were not the only threat to RAWA in Pakistan. The president, Zia ul Haq, was increasingly caving in to the demands of Mullahs for stricter and stricter application of *Sharia* Law, called in Pakistan the *Hudood*. Women in Pakistan were imprisoned for running away from their husbands, even in cases where the husband battered the wife. Even a twelve-year-old wife could be jailed for leaving a much-older husband she had not chosen. Pakistan courts routinely jailed women who went to the police to report they had been raped. Without four male witnesses to the rape who would testify, the woman could be charged with fornication or adultery. The testimony of women and non-Muslims was worth less in court than the testimony of Muslim men.

When Meena fled, she escaped the war and the Soviets, but she ran into the jaws of one of the world's regimes most repressive to women.

She went first to Peshawar, due east of Kabul, where she joined her husband, Faiz. By 1982, 1.7 million Afghan refugees had swelled this border city in Pakistan to a vast warren of camps with tents and makeshift shanties spreading for miles around.

Faiz's group was holding on, trying to contribute to the war against the Soviets. Many of the youthful leftists like the Maoists had abandoned their small parties and joined the *mujahedeen* to fight with one or another of the anti-Soviet armies. Faiz, and those in his group who remained, tried to support them with medical and other aid. Peshawar was the best place to do that, but in the atmosphere of the warlord-dominated refugee camps, their secularist and leftist political views had to be concealed.

Meena stayed only a few weeks in Peshawar before she realized that her work would be far too restricted in a place so tightly controlled by the rule of the warlords. Organizing for RAWA would be nearly impossible. She decided that even though it meant leaving her husband, she would move south to the more open border city of Quetta, the wild and lawless capital of the province of Baluchistan.

When Meena first went to Quetta, it was a city of about half a million people, which soon swelled to over a million. Huge camps spread over the rocky ground where Afghan refugees raised their flimsy tents and cardboard shanties. Each camp fell under the rule of a warlord of a different faction.

Meena was shocked to see the miserable conditions in the camps, where the people were trying to survive with only the barest supply of water. Cemeteries around the camps were filled with the graves of the countless children who did not survive the disease, hunger, and exposure of life in them. More graves held the many women who died in childbirth. Tattered flags fluttering in the wind marked the graves of the thousands of *shaheeds*—martyrs—who had fallen in the war against the Soviets.

The hardest thing to find in the dry, dusty, tan-colored city of Quetta was a place to live with a real roof over one's head. Quetta is in the mountains, with severe winters. RAWA was able to find only a few small places to rent at first. The women crowded in, several sharing each cramped room.

Only a short time after Meena arrived in Quetta, Yelda followed her there. The high-school-aged RAWA member who wore glasses and long brown braids had been wanted by the police in Kabul ever since she passed out leaflets for the April 1980 demonstrations. Yelda had been forced to live in hiding in Kabul. Meena had never met Yelda, but she had known about her for years. She sent a message, through the RAWA members working with Yelda, to reassure Yelda and her family that if she decided to leave for Pakistan, she would have care and a place to stay. It would not be a defeat to leave the country, Meena explained. It was a tactical retreat, to allow them to work harder for freedom.

Reluctantly, Yelda decided to go. She simply could not live in confinement any longer. Sadly, she said good-bye to her family and, accompanied by a RAWA guide, took the long and exhausting journey to the southeast, through Kandahar and across the mountains to Quetta.

Yelda joined three other RAWA members in a crowded and shabby little house. She struggled through her first discouraging week in Quetta, trying to adjust to the unfamiliar streets, and the dust. Yelda and her housemates barely had adequate food, and even reliable clean water was a problem. In most ways, they were like any other ordinary refugees, forced to seek safety from a war. Lonely and disoriented, far from home and family, without work or comfort, they had dim prospects for a future. There was only one thing different about them: They had RAWA. They were connected to each other and to a vision of doing something to help other Afghan women.

Yelda was told that someone would come to talk to her about her work. She thought it would be another RAWA member. She had heard about Meena, but she had never seen her.

Then Meena walked into the modest little room where the RAWA women ate. For Yelda, the moment froze. Before her was a beautiful woman dressed in the simplest old clothes, and wrapped in a cheap *chador*. Meena kissed and hugged Yelda as if she had always known her, and asked her about her journey. Meena told Yelda to forget about work for a while because she was tired and must rest. Yelda felt welcomed and loved. Meena was only twenty-five years old; but to the refugee girls like Yelda, she was like a mother.

Yelda next saw Meena when she came to meet with the four young women living together. She asked them, "What do you think about creating literacy courses for the refugees?"

Meena thought learning to read would help the refugee women, and also help RAWA to recruit new members. If RAWA hoped to get anything done, Meena told them, they had to become stronger.

The young women agreed to start literacy courses. They found some refugees who welcomed the chance to join in and learn. Many sent their children to RAWA's classes.

RAWA restructured to operate in two nations. Meena and one other senior leader were in Pakistan, the rest in Kabul. They maintained contact by making the dangerous journey back and forth, carrying smuggled messages.

Meena's secret journeys were now in reverse—from exile, she made brief, dangerous forays back into her homeland—at least two trips each year, sometimes three. She needed to see the other leaders and assess the needs of the members in Kabul.

Thoughts of her little daughter were never far from Meena's mind, and she, too, drew Meena back to Kabul. Mowaish had moved with her daughters to the Soviet-style high-rise apartment complex near the Kabul airport. Meena's baby had grown into a chubby, healthy toddler who played with the many other children in the apartment project. No one suspected she was not Mowaish's little girl. She was happy in her all-female household, spoiled and coddled by her doting big sisters.

When Meena was in Pakistan, Mowaish made sure Meena knew about her daughter's progress. She sent photos and tape recordings of her voice to Pakistan with RAWA members.

The planning and arrangement of border crossings was a major problem. Guides had to be paid, and guards bribed; papers falsified, letters of permission and visas obtained from officials, some of them friendly, some of them corrupt. RAWA spent a great deal of time cultivating relationships with the people who could make the passage safer for them.

Meena disguised herself so skillfully, sometimes even her friends did not recognize her right away. One of her favorite ways to dress for border crossings was as a *Gandi Wala*—one of the poor smuggler women who plied the mountains, paying off patrols with some of their merchandise. Meena colored her hair and wore scratched old eyeglasses. She wrapped herself in a tattered *chador* and put a bag of fabrics or trinkets on her back. With the shuffling gait of a much older woman, she walked the long miles into Afghanistan.

When RAWA wanted to move large groups of people over the border—students coming out to go to their schools, or medical workers traveling back and forth, they organized group crossings. Meena went along as a member of what looked like a big family, with many children and old people along. Once, Meena walked over the border pretending to be a member of a wedding party of over twenty people.

The RAWA women were forever devising clever ways to hide secret items. They concealed messages, forged documents, and copies of *Payam-e-Zan* in compartments in thermoses, radios, coconuts, suitcases, and inside the doors and engines of trucks.

The journey became more perilous as the war expanded. Meena and her companions were walking with a guide one night through a no-man's-land in the mountains when shots were fired very close by. The RAWA group ran, and scrambled down between some rocks. They realized they were in the cross fire between a contingent of Soviet soldiers and *mujahedeen* freedom fighters. There was nothing they could do but wait where they were, pressing themselves flat in the gravel and dust. When the firing died down, Meena sent the guide back to contact the *mujahedeen* commander. She told him to ask the commander to give the women guns, because they wanted to help in the battle. The fight did not last long enough for that to happen. But the commander and some of his men climbed down to meet these amazing women who had offered to help them. The commander ordered his men to escort them on their way.

Nearly every Afghan family was affected by the war, and many were torn apart. Millions fled into exile. Conditions grew so hard for Meena's parents in Kabul that, eventually, she brought them to Pakistan. Meena's mother, Hanifa, was her strongest supporter. She moved to Quetta and lived close to Meena. Meena's father settled in Peshawar near other relatives. Two of Meena's younger sisters also joined RAWA in Pakistan.

Like most Afghans whose loved ones were scattered, Meena could only hope that one day her family would be reunited.

12

WOMEN'S WORK

The refugee women in RAWA's classes kept telling their teachers that they needed income more than they needed to know how to read. Many could not see what use books were to them when they could not feed themselves or their children. Quite a few women knew how to sew and brought their mending to class. When Meena observed this, she conceived the idea of starting a sewing workshop. She began to recruit women who wanted to work in it.

Meena met Naheed, a pretty, green-eyed twenty-four-year old, newly arrived from Kabul, the single mother of a three-year-old son. She told Meena her story.

First, Naheed's brother-in-law had been jailed. Then one by one all the men in Naheed's husband's family were jailed or disappeared. Then, to save himself, Naheed's husband ran away, abandoning her and her son.

Naheed stayed behind in Kabul alone, caring for her son and her husband's three young sisters. The oldest girl, a tenth-grader, was the only one going to school. She met some members of RAWA, and joined.

One night, there was a knock at the door. Naheed's tenth-grade sister-in-law jumped up and grabbed some RAWA papers she had. Panicked, she thrust them into Naheed's hands, who stuffed them down into her clothes and opened the door. There were police all around the house, even up on the roof. They ordered everyone outside into the back courtyard and ransacked the house, but they didn't search Naheed's body.

After that, police came back about once a month to search. They never found anything, but Naheed was certain she and the girls would be arrested soon. She took what she could carry and went with the children to her widowed father. She left the girls with him, and then with her son made her way to Pakistan to see if it would be possible for her to survive there with the children. Her tenth-grade sister-in-law told her how to contact Meena through a RAWA member in Quetta.

Meena assured Naheed the whole family could come to Quetta and be safe. Naheed wanted to go back right away for the girls, but Meena said, "No, you are too tired, and it's too dangerous. There is an older lady who can travel much more safely. Let her go to get them all. She knows the way, and she is less likely to be attacked. If they are stopped, she can say the three girls are her granddaughters."

Naheed had no idea how her family would live. She was illiterate and unskilled, and had no money at all. Meena asked her if she could sew.

Naheed was not really good at it, and she admitted as much to Meena. Meena laughed, and said, "If you'll try, I'll bring you some fabric."

Naheed sewed some clothes that Meena praised. When Naheed's family of girls arrived from Kabul, Meena rented a little house for them and brought them three sewing machines. Soon, they were able to pay their rent themselves. As the sewing business grew, so did Naheed's confidence. Eventually, she began to teach sewing to other refugees, and everyone called her Naheed the Tailor.

Meena recruited fourteen women eager to sew. She found and rented a space where they did their work, and several of them lived together. The seamstresses decided the best item to sew for sale would be *Shalwar Kameez*—the loose pajama-type pants and matching long shirt that both men and women wear in Pakistan.

A lot of the refugee women already knew how to embroider. Meena recruited a tailor to come from Afghanistan to teach them to sew. Yelda even learned to cut patterns. After six months, they were all tailors. They sold the garments to shop owners who did not know they were sewn by RAWA members. The income not only paid all of the tailors, but also supported the literacy teachers.

Meena told them, "This one little project is paying for your family and for schools for other children and many other things to help refugees."

The greatest need in the refugee camps was for homes for young children. Many were war orphans, living with distant relatives or foraging in the streets. Thousands more lived with widowed mothers who could barely feed them.

Meena raised funds to rent two large adjacent houses with a courtyard between them, where RAWA opened a home and school for children. On her journeys to Afghanistan, Meena brought the children of RAWA members and supporters to the relative safety of Pakistan, where they could be enrolled in the school.

When she visited in Kabul, Meena stayed in touch with Basera, the young Tajik RAWA member who was still living with her family and studying science in high school. When Basera graduated, she was offered a scholarship to Russia, but she didn't want to go. How could she accept a Soviet award after they had killed her father and uncles?

"Basera, I think you should go," Meena urged her. "Your asthma is serious, and in Russia you can get medical care you can never get in Kabul or in Pakistan." Besides, Meena pointed out, Basera could discreetly try to protect other Afghan youngsters in Russia from being indoctrinated by Soviet education. Basera agreed to go.

She was sent to a small Russian city to learn the language. The school did not allow the Afghan students to go home for holidays. Basera was terribly homesick and unhappy there. Then the government sent her to Moscow to study chemistry. The only good thing for Basera was that her asthma dramatically improved.

Then a cryptic letter from home told her that her mother and sisters had left Kabul. Basera pieced together that they had fallen under police suspicion and had quickly left for Pakistan to join Meena. She later learned that two other girls they knew, members of RAWA, had been arrested because their house was searched and some anti-Soviet books were found. The girls' two brothers were also taken. One was executed. When the other was released, he was mentally ill from the trauma of his captivity.

Basera asked her teachers for permission to go back to Kabul to visit, but her request was refused, because, they said, it would cost too much to send her. Basera boldly told them she was leaving the program and going home. She went on her own by train and bus to Kabul, arriving at the end of 1983. She then made her way over the road and mountains to Quetta.

Basera moved in with her own family in Quetta. She joined her mother and sisters in meetings with Meena, who led them in study and discussion of the political situation. They all read *The History of Afghanistan* by the Afghan author Hobod. Meena led discussions of the worldwide women's movement. She also explained the ideas of the fundamentalist extremists to them. She told them of Gul-baddin Hekmatyar's past, of his involvement in the murder of a beloved poet. "If these men ever take power, things will be even more terrible in Afghanistan," she said.

There were only a few hundred RAWA members in 1983 in Afghanistan and Pakistan combined, but their impact was great. They alone kept alive the idea of women's freedom in a dark time.

To Meena, a major goal was the education of refugee children. She wanted to open schools for both girls and boys that would teach basic skills, along with democracy, women's rights, and science.

Meena was able to raise funds to open two *Watan* schools—one for boys and one for girls, in Quetta. *Watan* means "homeland" in Farsi. It was essential to educate boys, who were in danger of being recruited into the ranks of the fundamentalist ideologues who har-rassed and threatened RAWA in the refugee camps. These schools taught about democracy, and Afghan history. They were free for the students, and included grades 1–12. Geography, English, math, chemistry, physics, and the Pashtu and Dari languages were also taught. At their peak, 500 boys and 250 girls attended. There were more boys because it was much easier to convince refugees to educate their sons than their daughters. RAWA strove to provide a progressive education to every Afghan child sent to their schools. The girls' school was named *Nasima Watan*, in honor of an Afghan woman who was killed while bringing food to *mujahedeen* fighters.

Meena told all of the RAWA members she did not want any of them to be limited to just one vocation. "I want each one of you to be nurses and teachers, cooks and tailors. You all must be prepared to survive." Meena told them, "Today you have somewhere to sleep. Tomorrow, you might not."

Basera became a science teacher in RAWA's schools. She also learned Urdu, the main language spoken in Pakistan, and her responsibilities grew to interpreting for refugees with Pakistani doctors. She helped to deliver babies and became a midwife.

Meena constantly struggled to raise money internationally for the schools by writing to supporters in Europe and North America. But the bulk of the funds for the schools was earned by the sewing workshops, which by 1983 employed eighteen seamstresses.

Meena's fund-raising task was made harder by the corruption rampant in the refugee camps, where high percentages of international aid donated to help the refugees never reached them. Afghan families lived in squalor in the filthy, overcrowded camps while the warlords who ruled them built palatial villas with the money they siphoned from aid funds. Meena was determined that RAWA would set an example: Every cent would go to help the poorest of the poor.

RAWA's schools were an expression of Meena's belief that education was the answer to the spread of extremist and unscientific views. A generation of Watan graduates began to form the core of a more youthful RAWA that could take it into the future.

To Meena, the battleground was education. The fundamentalists' religious schools for boys, the *madrassas*, were able to take in far more students. Funded by Saudi oil money, the *madrassas* taught rote memorization of the Koran in Arabic, and the most extremist interpretations of it: an antisecular, antifemale doctrine, focused on hatred of Westerners and modernity.

At great risk to herself, Meena led RAWA to publicly oppose the fundamentalists. RAWA distributed leaflets and even held meetings in the refugee camps, exposing the crimes of the extremists.

Meena publicly asked questions: "Why have these men been chosen to oppose the Soviets? Why are they the people who have been picked to represent Afghans? Why are they supported by the United States, Saudi Arabia, Pakistan, the United Kingdom, and many other nations?"

Meena refused to choose among their warring factions. She boldly labeled all of them "misogynistic, antidemocratic, anticivilization, terrorist organizations, supported by foreigners to Afghanistan."

The extremists in return delighted in harassing the women of RAWA, trying to slander them in the camps by calling them whores, lesbians, communists, and "un-Islamic." They taunted RAWA members, yelled at them, threw rocks at them and sent them death threats. The RAWA teachers nevertheless bravely showed up day after day at RAWA schools.

Meena constantly warned about the warlords' terrifying record on human rights. In spite of RAWA's efforts, the stereotype of an Afghan freedom fighter became a bearded young man in a turban, carrying an automatic rifle. Women who labored daily in the camps, tending to the needs of refugees and educating Afghans about human rights, had no public image at all. Nor did they have funds. None of the American or Saudi money was used to strengthen democratic forces. Meena often said, "If we had the money the fundamentalists have, we would be able to educate every Afghan child."

All of the RAWA women worked endlessly. Yelda worked in the sewing shop in the morning. She studied nursing all afternoon and taught school at night. Most of the seamstresses worked part-time in the sewing business while also learning other skills.

Meena was so busy in Quetta, and the journey to Kabul had grown so dangerous, that her visits there were less frequent. Sometimes months passed with no contact between her and Mowaish. Meena's daughter had grown into a talkative little girl. Mowaish was saddened to think that Meena and Faiz were both missing the precious milestones of her childhood—all the sweet things a little child says and does.

In Mowaish's mind, it would be better for the child and for Meena if they could be reunited. Mowaish was nearly old enough to be Meena's mother, and she felt capable of deciding what was best for her, and for her foster daughter. She felt it was her duty to bring them together. Without consulting Meena, who she knew would object, she began to save money for a journey to Pakistan.

In the spring of 1983, Mowaish flew with Meena's daughter to India. She surprised Meena by phoning from there to say she was on her way.

Their first meeting took place at the sewing workshop. The seamstresses all expected Meena to show a lot of emotion, and hug and kiss the child. But she didn't. She acted the way she did with all of the RAWA girls—loving and kind but reserved. She did not want to overwhelm the child. Meena was also aware that the reunion was being observed by other women who were away from their families, or even had lost their families, and she was sensitive to their feelings.

The little girl had been told she would meet her birth mother. But she didn't react with immediate love for Meena. It was obvious she was close to Mowaish. Although Mowaish told her, "Go to your mother," the girl held back. Mowaish stayed for a few days, but she had left her own daughters in Kabul, and she had to return to them.

Whatever Meena's apprehensions about taking on the full-time care of her daughter, she loved having her there. The child moved into Meena's house, which was shared with other women. The adjustment was hardest for the little girl. She had a photo of Mowaish, which she put under her pillow every night. She cried and cried with homesickness for the only home she had ever known, in Kabul. She said she wanted Mowaish and the sisters she had known all her life. Meena did her best to comfort the child, but Meena was so busy that arranging daily care for her was another on the long list of difficulties facing her.

Late in 1983, an urgent phone call came from Peshawar. Meena's father, Latif, had fallen ill, and was asking for her. He was in a hospital in Peshawar. Meena made the difficult journey north as fast as she could, and arrived to find him barely able to speak. She had always loved him. He told her, "I have saved my last breaths for you." Meena sat with him until he breathed no more.

Grieving, she returned to Quetta to help with organizing what seemed like a hundred projects at once. Every day, more refugees came, more wounded, homeless, and orphaned children arrived. No matter how much she did, there was always more to do.

In Kabul, Mowaish's own daughters were so sad to have lost their little sister, they could barely eat or sleep. Conditions in Kabul were harder and harder for Mowaish. She was afraid her daughters would be raped by the soldiers who filled the city. Finally, after a year, the two mothers worked out a solution. Mowaish moved to Quetta, bringing her daughters with her. They all moved into a home with Meena and their shared child.

The house was very small, but to Mowaish it was full of love, and she was happy that she and Meena were working together. Asifa moved in, too. There were plenty of hands to help with the children.

Mowaish told Meena, "I brought all of these girls to you so that they can learn your way!" The girls were all enrolled in one of RAWA's schools during the day, and Mowaish worked in the tailor shop alongside two of her older daughters.

Mowaish, always the mother, was concerned about Meena's marriage. One day alone with her, Mowaish said to Meena, "You've only been married a few short years, but I never see you with your husband. I really want to see the two of you together because I love both of you. I always see you in different houses, and this makes me very sad."

Meena responded, "We do visit one another, but we have many differences."

Mowaish asked, "What differences?"

"Political ones," Meena said. "He has his ideology, and I have mine. Our work makes us live separately. We have different organizations."

Mowaish argued, "But this is your youth, and it makes me sad not to see you together."

Meena answered, "Sometimes I think it might be painful to the end of our lives, because as husband and wife, we love each other. But these political issues will keep us apart."

Mowaish cried for Meena that day, and asked herself, "What kind of life are they leading?"

Meena's seizures, which seemed to be exacerbated by extreme stress, continued to plague her. One day she was at home with Mowaish waiting for a phone call. RAWA was waiting to hear if several of their members who had been arrested were going to be released that day. The call came with bad news—their release would be indefinitely delayed. While talking on the phone, Meena had a seizure. Mowaish put water on her face, and in a minute she revived. Everyone felt concerned for her. It was a paradox that the strong leader they all relied on was vulnerable to collapsing without warning at any time.

Meena loved having her daughter living with her. Mowaish took care of her day-to-day needs, and Meena spent as much time with her as she could, reading stories to her if she came in before her bedtime. When she turned five, she was enrolled in one of RAWA's schools. She was still attached to Mowaish, yet when Meena had to leave, the little girl would cry.

"Why are you going, Mama?" she would ask tearfully. Meena would kneel beside her, and say, "Even though other things take so much of my time, I love you more than anything."

Now, when Meena had to leave her, it was to make the journey once more to Afghanistan. RAWA members repeatedly criticized Meena for taking risks. They would say, "Someday we could lose you." Yet she refused to bow to danger. Every time she made the trip back into Afghanistan they said good-bye as if it were the last time.

RAWA organized Meena's border crossings with as much care as possible. Once, she rode lying in the backseat of a car, covered with a *burqa* and also blankets, pretending to be so ill that she was close to death and unable to speak or open her eyes. At the checkpoints, the other people in the car told the officers that they were taking Meena back to Afghanistan to die. They were waved through.

When Basera, the Tajik midwife, arrived at Meena's house to start off with her on a journey to Afghanistan, she found Meena playing with her daughter. Meena hugged and kissed the little girl and said good-bye. They paused outside, because tears were pouring down Meena's face.

"I'm not giving her the love a mother should," Meena said, "because I've chosen a path where I could be killed at any time, and it would be too painful for her to lose me."

Meena never felt she could put either herself or her child ahead of others. One day Basera was working with Meena while her five-year-old daughter played nearby. The child picked up a little toy dog she found and was playing with it, but Meena took it away from her and put it away. The child cried and cried for it, and Basera asked Meena, "Why don't you give it to her?"

"Because it's not hers," Meena replied. "It was sent by some supporters in Europe for a child who is in jail with her mother. We have to take it to the prison in Kabul."

Basera said, "We'll just buy another one. Let her have it."

"No," Meena said. "Sometimes we have to put other children before our own."

The anti-Soviet war had raged in Afghanistan for five years by 1985. The refugee camps were vast cities of women, children, and old and wounded men, as the able-bodied men were nearly all fighting.

There still was no progressive, inclusive fighting force of Afghans. The war was led by the increasingly fanatic warlords whose infighting was barely held in check enough to fight the Soviets. Afghan secular patriots were given no sympathy by the Pakistani authorities, who left it to the Afghan armies to kill other Afghans as they wished. Afghan democratic forces were drowned out by the Islamists, who fought the war only as a war against atheism and communism, never as a war for democracy and human rights.

Meena and RAWA nevertheless put the need to throw the U.S.S.R. out of Afghanistan ahead of any other task. RAWA's highest priority was helping to fight the war. They continued to do everything they could to support the democratic *mujahedeen* who were fighting the Soviets. The *mujahedeen* had no access to medical care if they were wounded in Afghanistan. All they could do was to try to make it back to Pakistan. They often arrived hurt, exhausted, and starving. The RAWA members would drop everything to treat their wounds and feed them.

Meena cared very deeply about the men who were in combat. When a relative of a RAWA member came to Quetta fresh from battle, he was brought to Meena's house, exhausted and hungry. Meena went right out, borrowed some money from friends, and bought a chicken for him. Quickly she killed and plucked and cooked it. She made a kabob and fed him like her own child. Many said she treated the fighters like brothers, and cried for days when she heard one of them had been killed.

One day Asifa went with Meena to visit a refugee woman they both had known in Kabul. She had fled to Pakistan to join RAWA and escape the war. Her son, her only child, had joined the *mujahedeen* and had gone to fight the Soviets. She made one return journey to Afghanistan, where she was able to see him briefly. But when she went back inside the country a second time, she found his friends, who told her he had been killed.

Meena and Asifa bent low to enter her small tent in a long row of tents in a dusty camp street. The woman was prostrate with despair, lying on a pallet on the ground, another woman tending her.

"It happened in open combat with the Russian troops," she told Meena and Asifa. "His friends took me to the place where they buried his body."

Meena, bending over her, was so distressed, she was breathing heavily. Suddenly, she toppled forward, in a seizure. Asifa had seen this happen before, and she waited, stroking her forehead, until she came to. Meena remained lying down for a little while. "Sometimes I feel so small," Meena said in a weak voice. "The forces against us are so powerful." When Meena recovered enough to walk, they left, feeling utterly discouraged. That night, Meena cried so much that she rubbed the skin under her eyes raw.

Asifa frequently urged Meena to take time for her personal life.

"You've got to get away sometimes, spend quiet time with your husband and daughter."

But Meena answered, "Time might be short for us. We have to make the best use of it."

No one knew how often Meena and Faiz were together. Their meetings were brief and clandestine. Faiz never visited Meena's home, where Meena found her greatest pleasure in her daughter. When she returned very tired at night, she would crawl into bed next to her, and cuddle and talk. Some nights she told her stories, the kind of tales she had enjoyed as a child. But other nights, she began, "If someday I'm not with you . . ."

The child would object. "Stop, Mama. I don't like you to say that."

But Meena always repeated it. She would go on then to say, "You should not cry. You should know what I was doing and why."

Meena would explain her work to her child—the need to help women live good lives, the need to free their country from invaders.

The child would ask, "But why won't you be with me?"

Meena would answer, "Maybe I'll get sick, or die or in an accident or maybe an enemy will kill me. But you will be all right, because so many people love you and will take care of you."

In May 1985, Asifa and Mowaish were thunderstruck when Meena told them she was pregnant! This time, the roles were reversed. Asifa and Mowaish were worried about how she would manage, but Meena was happy and calm.

They were fighting a war, it was true, and conditions were very hard. But Meena felt she had the kind of support that would enable her to have another child. She was twenty-eight, her daughter was five.

As she did during her first pregnancy, Meena hardly slowed down. RAWA had so little money, the members walked everywhere. What little money they had for taxis was reserved for those members who were old or sick. But Meena never considered pregnancy an illness. She insisted on walking long distances. If she had to buy fabric for the workshop, she would walk all over Quetta to find the best price. The money was needed for the fabric, and she hated to spend it on a taxi. The seamstresses saw that she was tired, but she never admitted it, never complained. If she got to the workshop at mealtime, she would go into the kitchen and cook for everyone. If she saw the women were tired from the work, she would make them tea. Everyone told her, "You must rest," but she wouldn't. She was too busy even to sit down.

As the pregnancy advanced, Meena grew so large so early that Mowaish suspected she was carrying more than one baby. Sure enough, a visit to the doctor confirmed twins! Meena wrapped her bulk in a large black *chador* and continued to make her rounds to meetings, the sewing workshop, the schools. Naheed the Tailor had remarried, and she was pregnant, too. She couldn't see how Meena found her energy.

Meena was not a small woman. She was about five feet, six inches tall, and big-boned. But her own body grew thinner during the pregnancy, even though her belly was so big. At the end she was huge. Afghan women were considered immodest if they went out while very pregnant. Toward the end, she kept her arms folded in front over her big black *chador* in a futile attempt to conceal her belly.

Everyone made her tea and tried to get her to eat, to lie down, to go home. She brushed off the concern of the women around her. She would work long hours and stay until midnight sometimes, just as she had always done. When she got home, though, she would greet Asifa and Mowaish, ask how everyone was, laugh and tease them, but then she would lie down and pass out from exhaustion.

Everyone wanted to ask how Faiz felt about the twins, but when asked about him, Meena said little as usual. She answered simply that he was "fine."

As the birth approached, her doctor told her there was no adequate hospital in Quetta for the higher-risk birth of twins, and he advised her to go to Karachi. She told Mowaish, "No, I don't want to spend the money for the trip. Please use the money for something else." But all of the women gathered around her and gave her donations and insisted she take their money and go.

Faiz wanted to accompany her, but a journey to Karachi was far too dangerous for him. He remained in Peshawar, waiting for a phone call about the births. Meena left for Karachi with several women, one of them Mowaish's oldest daughter. The birth turned out to be completely normal, with no intervention needed. Meena returned to Quetta with two perfectly healthy babies, a girl and a boy.

Things would be different this time. Meena was determined to let herself mother these babies as she had never been able to mother her daughter. Though life in Quetta was hard, she did not have to be separated from any of her children. She let herself fall in love with the twins. She reveled in the relaxed time she spent nursing, gazing into the hazy eyes of her babies.

Naheed gave birth to a son at the same time the twins were born. She didn't have enough milk for him, and he was malnourished. Meena had plenty of milk from nursing twins, so two or three times a week, Meena pumped her milk with a hand breast pump and sent a bottle of it for Naheed's son.

Meena—super intellectual, super political leader—transformed into a super mother for a few brief weeks. Her first-born daughter was delighted with her baby sister and baby brother, and she and Meena spent happy, cozy hours admiring them. Though no one asked the details, Meena's closest confidants knew that Faiz came to spend time in some safe place with her and their children during this respite, their happiest time together as a family.

13

IRRETRIEVABLE
LOSS

When Meena returned to work she found places for the twins to be cared for where she was able to see them frequently. She left her little son with his grandmother Hanifa during the day, but two babies were too much for the old woman, so to the delight of the seamstresses, Meena's baby girl was brought to one of the sewing workshops each day. She had eight "mothers." None of the younger girls was married, so they joked that they were practicing on Meena's baby. The seamstresses took turns dressing and washing her, feeding her solid food and giving her bottles. Each day, one of the seamstresses was responsible for baby care. Best of all for the seamstresses, they saw more of Meena, because she came by often to nurse her tiny daughter.

One day, crawling on the floor, the baby picked up a metal staple, put it into her mouth, and choked on it. The seamstresses all panicked. They started crying, not knowing what to do. The baby was turning blue when Meena walked into the workshop. Meena calmly took the baby, stuck her finger down her throat, and carefully pulled the staple out.

Sometimes, when Meena came and took the baby girl away for a few hours, the seamstresses guessed that she was taking the twins to meet their father. Otherwise, the baby spent her days in the sewing shop. Meena would say, "I can hardly stand to leave her, but when I'm away from her, I'm so busy I don't have time to miss her."

Meena was an educator and administrator, but she also functioned as an all-around social worker. When a RAWA member's male cousin was about to be married in 1985, Meena intervened. It was an arranged marriage. The seventeen-year-old bride's illiterate, old-fashioned father was demanding 100,000 Afghanis in cash—a sum that, for many Afghans, is equal to their income for a year.

The father of the groom came to Meena to ask her for a loan to pay for the girl. The custom of bride-price had been dying out in Afghanistan, but in rural villages it was still paid, and some refugees still practiced it. Although she had never met them, Meena went to talk to the bride's family. She told the father, "You are selling your daughter like an animal. The bride-price will ruin the life of the couple, because they will have to borrow it, and so they will have to pay it back." She went to both sides again and again, negotiating. In the end, they all agreed not to have a bride-price, and to celebrate with a simple inexpensive wedding ceremony. When it came to convincing people to change their ways, no one was more persuasive than Meena.

Meena's favorite duty was to visit RAWA's children's homes. She loved her individual meetings with each child, and she paid special attention to those who had no living parents. She tried to learn all the children's names, but there were too many. She would say, "Come here, love," or, "Come here, darling," and then ask their names again. The children all came running when she arrived.

In 1986, six-year-old Shafika and her younger sister arrived in Quetta. Shafika's father was a doctor who had lost one of his legs in the war. Her mother was a housewife. Both of them were RAWA supporters living in Kabul. They sent their little daughters to safety in Quetta, to live in a RAWA home where they could be educated.

Shafika arrived, tired and frightened, at the unfamiliar *Watan* boarding school where thirty children lived and studied. Two large houses inside a walled courtyard contained sleeping dorms and classrooms. The teachers lived there, too, and everyone ate together.

On the second day Shafika was at the home, the children were told "Aunt Meena" was coming. Meena was famous for her punctuality. If she had said she would come at a certain time, she arrived exactly at that minute.

Meena noticed Shafika right away because she was new. She said, "Come here, sweetheart." She took Shafika onto her lap. Shafika had beautiful long, thick hair. A teacher had told her that her hair might have to be cut short, because it was hard to wash and comb it.

The first thing Shafika said to Meena was, "I don't want my hair cut. My mother used to comb it at home." Meena stroked her hair and admired it. She said, "Of course no one will cut such beautiful hair." She asked the principal to tell all the teachers not to give Shafika a haircut. The next time she came, Meena brought Shafika some special shampoo and a nice little hat.

The children who were not orphans went to visit their mothers in the nearby refugee camps on Fridays, but the orphans and those whose parents were far away, like Shafika, had to stay at the home. Meena sometimes arrived unannounced on Fridays to visit the left-behind children. When her driver pulled the car up in front of the home, she scooped the children into her arms and piled them into the car. "Come on," she said. "We're going on a little excursion, just to have some fun!" She sat in the back with Shafika and her sister and the other little ones, and teased and tickled them and laughed. "Take us to the candy store!" she told the smiling driver. The children knew it was not safe for Meena to be recognized in public. Inside the store, she pulled them all close around her, and little Shafika, pressing herself tightly against Meena's side, imagined she was protecting Meena from harm.

Once during Shafika's first year as a refugee, RAWA members took her and her sister on the long journey back to Afghanistan to see their parents. Shafika and her sister wrote letters to Meena, sending them back to Pakistan with a messenger, telling her how much they missed her. When Shafika saw Meena again at the children's home in Quetta, Meena bent down to tell her, "Thank you for your nice letter to me. You are such a good girl and a very good writer."

In 1986, RAWA decided to try to expand their work north to Peshawar. Meena thought RAWA was strong enough to attempt to work in the stronghold of the fundamentalists. That year, Osama bin Laden established his first training camp in Pakistan for his network of fighters that supported *Jihad* or Holy War against secular governments of the Muslim Middle East and the Western powers. Peshawar was a dangerous place, but so many refugees were there, Meena felt it was important for RAWA to have a presence.

Asifa moved to Peshawar to open a RAWA children's home there. Some of the Quetta seamstresses followed her to start a sewing workshop.

Meena's household changed. Asifa had gone to Peshawar, and Mowaish also moved, to Rawalpindi, where there was a growing population of refugees. Mowaish took on the job of travelling back and forth between Rawalpindi and Quetta, taking the clothes from the tailor shop in Quetta to sell, and bringing the money back to Quetta. Mowaish could travel a little more safely within Pakistan, because she was an older woman. Mowaish's daughters and Meena's daughter, now six years old, all stayed in Quetta, going to RAWA schools.

Meena had more than enough support to take care of the girls and pursue her most important new project: Malalai Hospital. RAWA had run mobile clinics in the past, but Malalai would be a real hospital—a long-held dream for RAWA. Malalai would treat land mine and bomb victims, deliver babies, and save the lives of sick women and children. It was a major undertaking, but Meena, always careful not to take on anything RAWA could not do, was sure the organization had grown strong enough to pull it off. She had raised funds from international donors and had found a building in Quetta. Meena and others were engrossed in the exhausting work of renovating the space and purchasing all of the equipment.

Then, on a November day in 1986, someone came from Peshawar with terrible news for Meena: Faiz had disappeared. Soon, friends there were able to find out that he had been abducted by members of the *Hezb-e-Islami*—Gulbaddin Hekmatyar's band of fundamentalists.

For a few days, Meena stopped everything. She did not come to work at all. She said she had stomach problems. She waited alone at home. It was not long before the final piece of news came: Faiz was dead. The information was that he had been tortured to death and that Gulbaddin Hekmatyar was involved.

Meena had never talked much about her husband or her marriage to most RAWA members, mostly for security reasons and partly to protect her privacy and his. Now, Meena had joined the ranks of the thousands of Afghan widows. She had comforted and aided countless widows in the past, and she had their example to guide her. She had seen bereaved women care for their children, and survive. She could expect no less of herself. To encourage the women of RAWA who looked to her, Meena hid her own despair.

Faiz's own organization did not at first announce his disappearance or death, so she could not even tell any but her closest confidantes what had happened.

Meena wanted to pull her daughter close to her as never before, but she had to separate from her, for the little girl's safety. Meena was afraid that the men who had killed her husband might also try to attack her and her daughter. She could not bring herself to tell her six-year-old that her father was dead, at the same time that she was sending her away. Meena sent her to Mowaish in Rawalpindi, to the "other mother" the child also loved. Meena made the decision not to tell Mowaish that Faiz was gone, so that her daughter could live in a happy home for the time being.

In her loneliest hours, she allowed herself to weep, and try to face the fact that her beloved daughter and her seven-month-old

twins were among the thousands of Afghan children who would
grow up without their fathers.

At least with her daughter gone, Meena did not have to try
anymore to conceal her grief-stricken face from the little girl.
Meena increased her own security, never going out without male
supporters with her. Like nearly all women in Pakistan, she had
always traveled in cars with a male driver. Now she added a bodyguard.

After some days of seclusion, Meena asked Basera and two other
members to meet with her to talk about the sewing projects. At the
end of the meeting, Meena told them that terrible news had come.

"A good man, one of our male supporters all of you have heard
about, has been killed by Hekmatyar's organization," she said. She
did not tell them the name of the one who was gone. The women
all started to cry. Meena told them, "You cannot bring him back
by crying. We have to use our energy to work to stop the killing,
because these men are murdering many, many other people. Turn
your grief into positive energy. Try to use this to become braver
and stronger."

Not long afterward, Faiz's group, the Afghan Liberation Organization, announced that he had been betrayed by a spy commissioned
by Gulbaddin Hekmatyar, and handed over to Hekmatyar's *Hezb-e-
Islami* henchmen. His body was not recovered.

Only then did Naheed and Basera realize that Meena had told
them about her own husband's death. Basera marveled at Meena's
bravery and control. If Meena had broken down, all of them would
have felt defeated and afraid. No matter what Meena herself was
suffering, she always thought of the example she was setting for
them.

All of the women noticed that Meena was quieter now. Some-
times they saw her deep in thought. Meena did not cry or scream.
She often mentioned other people who were missing, but never
Faiz.

The only sign Basera saw of Meena's stress was a seizure she
had at the sewing shop. Meena was sitting down when suddenly

she slumped over. She was breathing heavily, and Basera realized she wasn't asleep—she was unconscious. The women laid her down and brought cold water to bathe her face. After a few minutes she came to. Meena said, apologetically, "Sometimes I'm just so tired, I faint. I'm fine, don't worry about me." Half an hour later, she left to go on her way.

Meena threw herself even harder into her work. Opening Malalai Hospital became her obsession. She took a hand in every detail. She oversaw the furnishing of the building and interviewed the new employees. She asked the seamstresses at the workshop to make the nurses' uniforms, and she even personally designed them.

Meena's way of leading had always been to *show* the women around her, as much as to tell them her ideas. Her actions were a deeper teaching to them of the essence of what she wanted them to understand. She saw that it might be years before RAWA would make progress toward their goals, but she wanted them to know how to survive.

Meena's answer to despair was to organize, and she did nothing differently now. How much easier it would have been to stop, to give up, to rest. But how could she? When so many were suffering, Meena felt it was her duty to keep hope alive. Even if going on without her partner of ten years felt too hard, she had three children, and a movement to live for.

On February 4, 1987, Meena was in Quetta, at home, when a message came. Those who were in the house have only a vague memory of what it contained. Some say a note was delivered; others remember a phone call. Some recall Meena saying that a woman had arrived from Afghanistan with letters from members and supporters inside the country. Others say the message to Meena told her that a member had been released from prison and had arrived in Quetta. In any case, Meena was very anxious to go out to meet a woman. She left hurriedly, in a car, accompanied by two men—a driver and one other male escort.

At the sewing workshop, preparations were under way for Meena's visit that afternoon. Several of the younger members were

playing with Meena's baby girl; Basera and Naheed were putting the finishing touches on the nurses' uniforms. Meena had said she would come at 4 P.M. to admire them. She was always perfectly punctual, so the women had tea ready for her. But she was late. Five o'clock came and they waited. Night fell. Still they waited. Naheed the Tailor began to weep.

14

WITH ALL THEIR STRENGTH

RAWA had only two phones in Quetta, one of them in Meena's house. The seamstresses called both phones over and over to ask for her. No one knew where she was. RAWA members fanned out to go to every possible place, every house where Meena could possibly be visiting. They asked every member and supporter to tell them when she was last seen.

Meena's mother Hanifa was in Rawalpindi visiting Mowaish, with Meena's baby boy. The baby girl remained with the seamstresses in Quetta. Several times Mowaish's phone rang: RAWA members asking for Meena. The callers did not say she that was missing, only that they wanted to talk to her. But Meena wasn't there. Neither Mowaish nor Hanifa had any reason to worry.

One day passed. Two. Meena was nowhere. Nor could anyone find either of the men—the driver and the bodyguard—who had left her house with her. Because of the dangers inherent in RAWA's communications, the word spread through the organization slowly.

Asifa, in Peshawar with several of the seamstresses, tried to call Meena at home in Quetta for two days, but no one answered. Afraid Meena's house was being watched, all of the members were staying away from it. Asifa became concerned, and finally she phoned one of RAWA's trusted friends in Quetta, a doctor with the International Relief Committee who helped in the refugee camps. He went to Meena's house but found no one at home. Finally, Asifa got a call from a RAWA member in Quetta, saying Meena and her two male aides had disappeared. After the terrible news was spoken, both women were silent on the line, and then began to weep. Asifa's mind reeled through all the many possibilities: Perhaps the Pakistani police took them, perhaps the fundamentalists.

In spite of their fears of the police, after several days the members made the decision to go to them. An imperious officer, who showed them no sympathy, told them he had nothing to tell them. He made a show of writing a report, but it was obvious he was going to do nothing.

The women were terrified that Meena and the two men were being tortured. The women knew that few people can stand up for long to torture. They feared that whoever had kidnapped them would force them to tell the names and whereabouts of RAWA's members and supporters. The women scattered, went even deeper into hiding, and waited for a possible attack. Hurriedly, they burned documents, some of them irreplaceable. Much of the history of RAWA, early leaflets and issues of *Payam-e-Zan*, and even the only copies of some of Meena's poems went into the fire.

The women waited fearfully, staying away from their homes. As the days passed and there were no raids on their homes or additional kidnappings, it became apparent that Meena had not betrayed RAWA.

Nevertheless, the organization was in confusion. Slowly, they tried to meet safely to talk about what to do. They had many hard decisions to make. The first was what to tell Meena's mother. Hanifa suffered from a heart condition, and she was frail. The women feared that if they told her Meena was missing, she would not survive. For the time being, they agreed to tell Hanifa that Meena had gone to Afghanistan.

Weeks went by, and still there was no word of Meena or either of the men. The women became so desperate that they decided they had to ask for Hanifa's help. Their only hope was that if Hanifa were to go to the police, they would take pity on a mother who was searching for her daughter and tell her what they knew.

A sad delegation of women went to Hanifa and told her that Meena had been missing for weeks. Hanifa cried, but did not collapse. With several members supporting her, she went to the police station in Quetta. She begged the same unsympathetic officer to tell her what had happened to her daughter. His answer was no. No information.

The organization began to fray under the pressure. Two of the founding members, frightened by what was happening, resigned from RAWA and left for Europe.

RAWA's remaining leaders felt that RAWA was all they had left, and they could not let it die. They had to have help, and they reached out to ask for it. They decided to try to contact women with whom they had worked years before.

Sadaf, the teacher, had lost contact with RAWA nearly three years before. By the time she was finally released from prison in Kabul in August 1984, two of the four RAWA women who had been locked up with her had already been let go. Sadaf did not know where they had gone. Sadaf said good-bye to the member who was still in the prison, and left with her daughter, who was nearly three. Sadaf, with her baby, had served two and a half years for distributing RAWA leaflets.

She had no place to go. She had no money, and did not know where her husband was. The only place she could think of to go was to her father's house. But she was with her father for only two hours when agents of the secret service, the KHAD, came to question her there. She knew she could not try to make contact with RAWA, because she might lead KHAD to them. She also knew no one in RAWA would come to her father's house, because KHAD agents were constantly watching it.

Sadaf could not get work as a teacher because she had been fired from her job when she was arrested. She had learned how to type in college, so she survived through typing jobs. Finally, Sadaf found a job teaching science and math at a boys' school. She hoped that RAWA would be able to get in touch with her, in spite of the war and the risks.

One day Sadaf was teaching when the classroom door opened and a visitor came in—a stranger—who handed Sadaf a letter and quickly left. Sadaf stepped outside to the courtyard and opened the note. The writer was an old RAWA friend of Sadaf's. The first part of the letter was an apology. The writer, who said she was in Pakistan, explained that RAWA had not been able to contact her before, and asked her forgiveness. She then wrote: "Meena is missing, and probably dead. We really need you now. Please come."

As if Meena were standing in front of her, Sadaf saw the vibrant and beautiful fifteen-year-old girl with the serious black eyes. Sadaf could not go back to class. She told the principal she had to leave immediately because of a death in her family.

She went home, and sitting alone thinking about the women she had known in RAWA, she decided to go to Pakistan immediately. She quit her job abruptly, took her five-year-old daughter, and followed the refugee roads and trails to Quetta, where she found the organization and its remaining leadership undergoing a profound crisis.

A group of RAWA's leading women gathered in a small room. Asifa embraced Sadaf. Asifa was so destroyed by grief that she had not been able even to weep. She admitted to the others that she was burning inside with anger toward herself and even toward Meena.

"She insisted on working so openly," Asifa said. "I should not have allowed her to expose herself so much."

"We all blame ourselves," someone else said. "Every one of us should have insisted that she hide herself more, especially after her face became known when she was in Europe. Think of all the times she went out in public bareheaded, or wearing just a scarf, when it should have been a *burqa*. Our enemies took advantage of our carelessness."

"But Meena was Meena," Sadaf said. "No matter what anyone said, she never would have stopped speaking out."

Everything was ready for the opening of Malalai Hospital. The doctors and nurses were ready to go to work, and refugees and war victims needed care. The women made the difficult decision to go ahead with it. "As hard as it is to open it without her, the hospital is the best monument to Meena," Asifa said. "She worked her heart out for it, and she would want us to keep going."

Malalai was open only two days before it filled with patients. Through the sweltering summer of 1987—the ninth year of the Soviet occupation—as more and more victims fell in the war's killing fields, the women of RAWA worked on.

In the frightening atmosphere of Pakistan's refugee community, where allegiances shifted constantly, it was hard to trust anyone, and no one ever felt truly safe. People who had not known Meena well were suspicious. Had she run away to an easier life in Europe? There were rumors that she had abandoned RAWA, and even that she had stolen some of RAWA's funds, or defected to RAWA's enemies.

Mowaish, Asifa, Sadaf, Basera, and many others knew none of it was true. Naheed and the other women in the sewing shop knew Meena would not have abandoned her children. They kept the baby girl with them in the workshop, praying Meena would appear.

Then in August, six months after Meena disappeared, without any warning, or even a phone call from the police, the women of RAWA read devastating news in the Pakistani newspapers. Two men, the articles said, had been stopped trying to drive across the border from Afghanistan to Pakistan. Their car had been searched and found to contain a large amount of explosives. They were arrested and had confessed, perhaps under torture, that they had killed three people: RAWA's two missing male supporters and a thirty-year-old woman named Meena.

To read that news item was horrifying beyond words for the women of RAWA. Though they had asked the police to inform them if anything was ever found out about Meena, no one from the authorities came to talk to them. They did not know whether to believe the newspapers. The articles did not say what target the men had been planning to bomb. All the women knew was that if the articles were true, Meena was dead.

Equally shocking, the articles said that one of the killers was a man well-known to RAWA. He was one of their male supporters, Ahmed Sultan. The articles said the other culprit was his cousin, Mohammed Hamayoun, a name no one in RAWA had ever heard.

Sultan and Hamayoun, the news items said, had led the police to two bodies buried in the garden of an empty house in Quetta. The address was a house that had once been rented by RAWA. Shortly before Meena had disappeared, the lease had expired. The members had moved out and left the place vacant.

To conceal the bodies, the killers had dug deep narrow, vertical holes straight down into the earth. They had put Meena's body in one, and the body of one of her male companions in the other. They had poured cement over the holes and placed planters on top to hide the place as a flower bed.

There were many unanswered questions. Where was Meena's other missing aide? His body was not found, and though the murderers said they had killed him, nothing was disclosed about what had happened to him.

The horror of Meena's end was almost more than her friends and family could bear. The fact that she was killed by someone who had gained access to her inner circle and who had known many of them was, of course, much worse than if it had been done by strangers. The women of RAWA had to cope all at once with the news that Meena was dead and with the sudden knowledge of the security disaster that had brought her killer into the heart of RAWA.

Mowaish heard the news from one of her own daughters. Mowaish was sitting on the *toshak* with Meena's six-year-old daughter, sewing. Mowaish's daughter came into the room carrying a picture of Meena. She broke down crying and said Meena was dead.

Mowaish held out her arms to the child, and said, "Thank God your father is alive for you."

At that point, Mowaish's daughter had no choice but to tell the whole truth. "No," she said, "three months ago, Dr. Faiz was also killed."

Meena's daughter went to the weeping Mowaish, put her head down on her lap, and sobbed.

Everyone in RAWA felt devastated, but the leadership had to take action. A delegation of RAWA members, Asifa leading them, went to the Pakistani police. Asifa hated to walk past the coldly staring police. She pulled her *chador* far forward over her hair and held the cloth tightly under her chin. The women were ushered into an office, where they stood before the same stern officer who had denied their earlier requests for information. Asifa said, "We have come to retrieve Meena's body, so that we can bury her properly."

"That will not be possible," the officer said. "If you were to bury her, someone would blow up the grave." It sounded like a threat. Asifa did not have time even to reply before he added, "The body has already been buried."

"Where is her grave?" Asifa asked.

"I cannot give you that information," he replied. "I can only tell you that the body is in a place where the authorities bury the unclaimed bodies of people who have been murdered."

Swallowing hard, Asifa persisted. "What can you tell us about how she died? We do not know what happened."

"At the time they were unearthed," he said, "the bodies, of course, were decomposed. The victims' hands had been tied behind their backs. Both of them had been strangled."

The officer then said, "A ring was recovered from the body of the woman. We have not positively identified her as Meena. Can one of you tell us whether Meena wore a ring?"

Asifa said she could recognize Meena's ring.

"Come with me," the officer said.

As Asifa walked down the stairs behind him, she realized that she was holding on to a shred of hope that it was all a mistake, that Meena was not really gone. In the basement of the building, Asifa stood in a dim hallway as the officer unlocked a closet that held numerous plastic bags of evidence, labeled with tags. He took out a small bag, shook a ring out onto his palm, and held it out toward Asifa. It was the inexpensive silver wedding band Meena always wore. Asifa reached out to pick it up, but the officer jerked his hand away and closed his fist over the ring. "This is evidence," he said. "You cannot have it."

Now the sad task of telling the youngsters living in RAWA's children's homes that Meena was gone could no longer be put off. Shafika, the girl with the beautiful long hair, was eight. She and the other children were called into the big room where they ate together. Gently, the teachers explained to them that Meena would not be coming back. She had been killed.

For many of the children, Meena's loss was a blow that came on top of the deaths of their own parents. The war was all they had ever known, and it seemed to reach them everywhere. Little Shafika, hearing Meena was gone, wanted her own faraway mother and father to come and hold her. The teachers held the children, talked with them, and helped them draw pictures of Meena and talk about their memories of her. They said prayers for her, and wept.

RAWA's leaders next had to find a new, permanent home with RAWA supporters for Meena's and Faiz's eighteen-month-old twins. The care of the little boy had become too much for Meena's ailing, widowed mother, Hanifa. The seamstresses tearfully said good-bye to the baby girl they had cared for since she was an infant. Meena's seven-year-old daughter remained safe with Mowaish.

The women closest to Hanifa agonized about whether to tell her Meena was dead. Feeling her heart condition was too serious, they decided not to tell her for the time being. They told her that Meena was safe in Afghanistan after all. Meena's youngest sister arrived from Afghanistan and made arrangements to take Hanifa to safety in Europe. RAWA paid the smuggler's fee for them to be taken illegally out of Pakistan to India, through the tightly controlled border with Kashmir.

But Meena's mother did not survive the journey. Hanifa and her daughter were on a bus crowded with Indian and Pakistani passengers. Such buses often carried people crossing illegally. The bus was stopped and fired upon by Indian soldiers at the border. Some people were killed, and Hanifa was wounded. Meena's sister was not hurt. She took Hanifa back to Lahore, Pakistan, to a hospital, where she died for lack of a blood transfusion.

In the face of this new sadness, the women in the leadership drew closer together, more determined than ever to save RAWA.

Their appeals to the Pakistani judicial system to bring the murderers to trial fell on deaf ears. Under the repressive *Hudood* laws, which did not recognize the rights of women, Meena's death was not even considered a crime. Even though they had confessed, the killers were not charged with Meena's murder. Nor were they even punished for killing Meena's two male aides. Because they were RAWA supporters, their murders were ignored. The killers were held in prison on charges of possessing a car bomb, but not for killing Meena and her two aides.

An even more bitter reality was the open jubilation of the extremists in the refugee camps. They celebrated Meena's death, calling out taunts to the women entering and leaving RAWA's schools.

Even some longtime friends of RAWA did not come forward to condemn Meena's murder—probably too afraid of retaliation to be associated with RAWA in its hour of sorrow.

Sadaf, Asifa, and the other leaders grew close, meeting again and again to honestly evaluate their situation. "Some people are saying that without Meena, RAWA will collapse," Asifa said.

"We cannot let that happen," Sadaf said. "In such a long struggle, we will make mistakes. This happened because of a terrible error we made. The thing now is to try to understand the mistake we made, and go on."

Sitting on cushions in the small safe room where they met, the women looked into each other's sad, shocked eyes, and together they faced what had happened. They had trusted a traitor.

RAWA's security policy had been gradually to get to know people through their associations with others they trusted. It was a delicate and subjective process, and in Ahmed Sultan's case, it had failed them. Sultan's sister was a trusted member of RAWA. When Sultan arrived in Quetta, his sister met with him, then slowly introduced him to other RAWA members. Meena needed an English translator; she spoke Farsi, Pashto, and French, but not English. She needed English for press conferences, and to speak to international supporters and donors. Ahmed Sultan was an educated, sophisticated man who had lived in Europe and spoke not only Farsi and English, but also Russian and Turkish.

"He seemed perfect," Asifa said. "But, really, we did not know him. We never should have allowed him to meet Meena."

After Ahmed Sultan was introduced to Meena, he was allowed into her inner circle as her translator. He became one of the men who escorted her frequently as her bodyguard. Only Meena herself knew her schedule. Usually, most members had no idea even whether she was in Afghanistan or Pakistan. Only a few people had ever been allowed to get really close to Meena—to know her movements and where she lived. Ahmed Sultan had been one of those few.

Even harder to face was the fact that Sultan and one of Meena's younger sisters had fallen in love. They planned to marry. Ahmed Sultan was therefore considered a member of Meena's family. No one had been suspicious of him, and no one had any way of knowing Sultan had a cousin, Mohammed Hamayoun, with ties to both Gulbaddin Hekmatyar and to the Afghan/Soviet secret police, the KHAD. This two-faced role was not unusual with Gulbaddin Hekmatyar's group, which is more like a well-funded criminal mafia than an armed political force. They are hired killers who have switched sides many times in Afghanistan's long nightmare of war.

When Meena disappeared, no one suspected Sultan. He had left for Kabul soon after. Meena's sister also returned to Kabul, where they quietly married. She, of course, had no idea she was marrying a man who had murdered her own sister.

"We sent members to try to talk to Meena's sister," Asifa said, "but they could not contact her." She lived with Sultan's parents in Kabul. His father kept her secluded behind the walls of their home, and refused to allow anyone to see her.

Sultan's sister, who had introduced Sultan to Meena, was also confined inside her father's house. No one from RAWA could talk to either of them.

The RAWA leaders in the meeting went over the many possible scenarios for how Meena's ambush was arranged. The killers could have been paid large sums to do what they did. One or both of them could have been threatened with death unless they carried out her murder.

Asifa declared, "I think that from this day forward, the only men we should allow to know our networks should have grown up in RAWA schools. Before they meet our leaders, we should have known them most of their lives." They all agreed to the new policy.

"The Pakistani police are doing nothing to investigate," Sadaf said. "Unless the men who ordered Meena's death and probably paid for it—the men behind Sultan and Hamayoun—are arrested and tried, we will never see the complete picture of what happened to Meena."

Asifa said, "Her death can't mean that we abandon our principles. I'm sure if we had been less outspoken against the fundamentalists or the Soviet puppets, we might still have Meena with us, but we have to carry on with the ideas she died for."

She insisted: "From the very beginning, RAWA's main goals were freedom, democracy, and social justice for everyone. We've never had any fear of talking about our beliefs. Meena gave us the confidence in ourselves to speak up, and we should still do that."

"Otherwise," Sadaf agreed, "there will be no nonviolent alternative to either the Russians or the fundamentalists. If we are quiet, there will be no democratic voice, and nothing but more violence."

They reread Meena's poems out loud to each other. One line from "I Shall Never Turn Back" spoke to them now more than ever: "With all my strength I'm with you on the path of my land's liberation."

"She is with us," Sadaf said. "We have her strength, and we will need all of our own."

15

RAWA RISING

Crying at times as they worked, the women of RAWA wrote and published *Payam-e-Zan*'s saddest issue, telling their readers about Meena's death.

With funds from international donors, they expanded Malalai Hospital to four doctors, eight nurses, lab and X-ray technicians, and a pharmacist. Malalai became known as the best place for victims of land mines to go for help.

Day by day, a new generation of educated Afghan children grew up in RAWA's schools and children's homes. Asifa, Sadaf, and the other leaders had managed to keep RAWA alive. The strength they forged together helped them through the hard times that lay ahead.

Not long after Meena's death in 1987, Mikhail Gorbachev, the new leader of the U.S.S.R., called Afghanistan "a bleeding wound that has to be stanched." Ponomarev, whom Meena had confronted six years before in France, and other Soviet hard-liners, opposed Gorbachev, but in the end they were brought down by the Afghan war.

Disillusioned, wounded, and traumatized Soviet veterans limped back to Russia as more and more Russian families refused to send their sons to the front. Soviet troops and secret agents, jets and helicopter gunships raining bombs and napalm down onto villages had not been enough to subdue Afghan guerrilla fighters and stop the resistance of the population.

Poster published by RAWA in late 1987, during the war of resistance against the Russians and their Afghan puppet government.

In the end, Gorbachev's view prevailed. On February 14, 1989, the last Soviet soldier left Afghanistan, leaving behind a shaky puppet regime headed by Mohammed Najibullah, and millions of land mines hidden in the earth. The economy was in ruins, the irrigation system and roads destroyed. A million and a half Afghans had been killed, and five million more driven into exile. No one knew how many amputees and mentally ill people were left behind. An estimated 1 million children had been orphaned.

Afghanistan had indeed been the Soviet Union's Vietnam, and a key to its undoing. Fighting and losing the war drained their economy and eroded the loyalty of the Russian people. Soon, the whole Soviet empire crumbled. In November 1989, crowds of people in Berlin pulled down the wall that had divided East from West. Many other pressures on Russia had pushed on that wall, including the nuclear disaster at Chernobyl, but Afghans had given it a strong shove.

There was no one to help Afghanistan rebuild and heal its wounds. The Soviet Union was gone, and the United States, which had no further use for Afghans as anticommunist fighters, turned its back on them. The number of news reports about Afghanistan in the world's press plummeted, along with funding for refugees.

In 1991, Iraq invaded Kuwait, and the resulting Gulf War diverted the attention of the people of the world. Afghanistan and Afghans were forgotten. In spite of the billions of dollars the Afghan warlords had taken from the U.S. and Saudi Arabia, they sided with the Iraqi dictator Saddam Hussein in the Gulf War.

The Soviet's Afghan puppet, Najibullah, was barely able to hold on to power in Kabul for two years after the Soviet withdrawal, as Afghanistan succumbed to a brutal civil war. The fundamentalist armies, each one headed by a rapacious warlord, constantly fought each other for power.

In 1992, the puppet president Najibullah was pushed out of Kabul. Rabbani, who had been a fundamentalist professor at Kabul University in the 1970s, set himself up as president of Afghanistan, but he was able to control only Kabul, with the support of his old student, Masood. Their old enemies, Gulbaddin Hekmatyar among them, fired rockets and missiles into Kabul neighborhoods continuously from 1992 to 1995, killing an estimated fifty thousand people and leveling large parts of the city. The warring factions looted Kabul. They even ripped out the entire electric bus system and sold it to Iran.

Every side in the civil war was guilty of war crimes, including repeated massacres of civilians. The people would never forget the names of the criminal warlords: Hekmatyar, Dostum, Sayyaf, Rabbani, and Masood. The warlords divided the nation into fiefdoms, and all of them fought, changed sides, and fought again in a free-for-all of bloodshed and betrayal. Rape, murder, highway robbery and theft, brutal executions, amputations, and kidnappings were the rule.

Gulbaddin Hekmatyar was one of the main culprits. He controlled an area east of Kabul, where he and his henchmen imposed

Nurses of Malalai Hospital teach Afghan women some basic
health-care methods in Quetta, 1989.

their frightful rule over the people. Throughout this terrible period,
which produced many more refugees, RAWA stood firm.

"As bad as it was," Asifa said, "we all felt that we had already
been through the worst when Meena died. It was as if we had
learned how to withstand anything."

International sources of funding for Afghan refugees shrank until RAWA could no longer even sustain the cost of Malalai Hospital
in Quetta. In 1994, in spite of the fact that the number of land
mine victims had not diminished, RAWA was forced to close Malalai for lack of funds.

RAWA shifted its medical aid back to small clinics. Basera the
midwife opened a RAWA clinic in a village inside Afghanistan,
where she also taught women how to read.

In Pakistan, RAWA continued to teach and heal refugees. RAWA
provided services in refugee camps where they set up schools, and

A RAWA literacy class for women in RAWA camps.

medical clinics were held weekly. Women in RAWA camps could go about bareheaded or wearing only small scarves. Less fortunate women and girls who lived in areas ruled by warlords had to try to sneak into RAWA's camps to learn to read or see a doctor.

The women of RAWA never stopped trying to tell the outside world what was happening to Afghanistan, but no one seemed to be listening. For six years, from 1990 to 1996, even the United Nations Security Council did not discuss Afghanistan. Afghans became the forgotten people.

Just as Meena had said many times, the silent battleground was education. With few resources, RAWA taught the poorest of the poor. In Quetta, thousands of homeless orphans roamed the streets, begging. Many collected garbage to sell in the hope of being able to buy a scrap of food at the end of the day. RAWA brought such orphans into their children's homes, fed them, and sent them to RAWA's schools, where they were taught to read and learned about democracy. RAWA provided help for hundreds of children.

But the *madrassas,* well funded by donations from conservative Muslims in Pakistan, Saudi Arabia, and other nations, indoctrinated many more homeless boys to hate the West and to follow the war-lords. For many displaced and traumatized boys too poor to survive otherwise, the *madrassas* offered food, shelter, and, especially for orphans, a sense of belonging somewhere. Thousands were taught that the followers of every other religion are the enemies of Islam, that there can be no peace between Christians, Jews, Hindus, and Muslims, and that democracy is against the tenets of the Koran. Absolute obedience to their teachers and the honor of dying in *Jihad*—Holy War—was drilled into them.

The vast majority of Afghan refugees were moderate Muslims. For them, *Jihad* has a deeper meaning; it refers to a religious per-son's sincere effort to live according to the highest teachings of the Muslim faith.

A young Afghan fundamentalist religious leader emerged from the *madrassas* named Mullah Omar. He organized some young men into a movement called the Taliban, which means "the students." At first, the group was small. But the sinister Pakistani secret police, the Inter-Services Intelligence, or I.S.I., saw in these militant stu-dents a force they could use to take over Afghanistan and extend Pakistan's power. The I.S.I. openly backed the Taliban, giving Mul-lah Omar guns and large sums of money to recruit thousands more men. Pakistanis and Arabs from many other Muslim countries joined the Taliban and were paid to fight in Afghanistan. Mullah Omar began to lead armed groups of Talibs into Afghanistan to join in the civil war. At first, their aim was to try to establish order by taking power from the warlords.

At first, the Taliban won the cautious support of the Afghan population, who were desperate to be rescued from the warlords. As the Taliban conquered more and more of Afghanistan, people welcomed them, hoping they would bring an era of just Islamic law and order to the war-weary nation. Thousands more *madrassa* students and volunteer fighters from other nations streamed across the border from refugee camps in Pakistan to join Mullah Omar's Taliban.

In 1996, the Taliban succeeded in driving the warlords out of

Kabul. Gulbaddin Hekmatyar fled into exile in Iran. Rabbani and his ally Masood retreated to northern Afghanistan. They later called themselves the Northern Alliance and kept up military resistance to the Taliban from their stronghold in the Panshir Valley.

To the horror of the Afghan people, as the Taliban and their Arab allies marched across Afghanistan, they imposed the strictest interpretation of Sharia law ever seen in the history of Islam, which many Islamic scholars called a gross distortion of their religion. The Taliban chased moderate and liberal Mullahs from the mosques and installed fundamentalist Mullahs to help enforce their rule.

The Taliban leaders preached ethnic hatred. Most of them were Pashtuns, and when they conquered the city of Herat, they massacred Hazaras and Uzbeks, leaving the streets filled with bodies.

As they marched into each area of Afghanistan, the Taliban closed down girls' schools and fired women teachers. They banned women from the universities. Women could no longer work anywhere outside their homes, not even in international aid agencies, which, one by one, reluctantly packed up and left the country.

Male doctors were forbidden to examine female patients. They were allowed to talk to women only if they were concealed behind a curtain. Women were banned from practicing medicine.

Basera, who had been delivering babies and teaching reading in a rural Afghan village during the civil war, had to close her RAWA-supported clinic and go back to Quetta, where she turned her attention to the needs of refugees.

In Afghanistan, the Taliban imposed almost total separation of the sexes. Women were forced to stay inside, and the windows of their houses had to be painted black, so that they could not see out.

In order not to "inflame the desires" of men, all women were ordered to be covered by burqa. The Talibs beat any woman who accidentally showed an ankle or a wrist. Women could not wear shoes that made a noise. White shoes or socks were banned, because white was the color of the Talib flag. Lipstick and nail polish were outlawed. Women were to speak in low voices.

Many Talibs, who professed to control women for their protection, now kidnapped and raped them at will. The Talibs took wives for themselves by force, even very young girls.

Meena's old friend Roya lost contact with RAWA during the years of the civil war. She survived the destruction of much of Kabul, only to face the abuses of the Taliban. When they arrived, Roya's husband, who was a teacher, lost his job. Roya, like other women, could not go out of the house for fear of being beaten or raped. So many Talibs demanded to marry Roya's older daughter that Roya feared they would forcibly take her, and so she, too, had to stay inside. To survive, Roya's husband sold vegetables from a cart in the street. As he and Roya had no sons, their younger daughter dressed as a boy and worked at the vegetable cart, helping her father.

Men were not exempt from the Taliban's cruelty. All men were ordered to grow beards, and they were beaten if their beards were too short. Prayer five times daily was mandatory. Even grandfathers too old to bow down were dragged out of their homes and forced to go to the mosques.

The Taliban even outlawed kite-flying, an age-old Afghan tradition. They banned all sports, and turned the soccer stadium into a public execution ground.

The Taliban left no doubt that they had declared war against the Afghan people, and even the Afghan land. As anti-Taliban farmers fled into exile, instead of using their farms, the Talibs cut down their fruit trees and burned their homes so that they would not be able to return. The Taliban had no concept of how to run an economy or provide for the people.

Other nations halted trade with Afghanistan, and famine began to spread. Rates of disease, malnutrition, mother and infant mortality climbed to new heights. Severe depression, other mental illnesses, and suicide increased sharply among both men and women.

The Talibs' cruelty arose out of the terrible conditions of the refugee camps. RAWA knew the Talibs were children of war, many of them orphans. Raised in all-male *madrassas*, most had known no mother, sister, wife, or daughter. They had had no real childhoods. They were so traumatized and indoctrinated that many of them seemed to know nothing but how to destroy.

When the Taliban first took power, the United States did not oppose them, because they were supported by Pakistan and Saudi Arabia, both U.S. allies. The U.S. ignored the Taliban's human rights violations, hoping they would oppose Iran, crack down on farmers who grew opium poppies, and allow an oil pipeline proposed by an American corporation, Unocal, to be built across Afghanistan. U.S. policy toward the Taliban did not shift until late in 1997, as the chaos in Afghanistan threatened to destabilize nuclear-armed Pakistan. Finally, Secretary of State Madeleine Albright publicly criticized the Taliban's suppression of women, calling it "despicable."

Out of sight of the world, Afghanistan and the lawless border area of Pakistan were the perfect hiding places for Osama bin Laden. In 1988, he had founded Al Qaeda—Arabic for the Base—a network of Islamic militants from numerous nations, dedicated to killing secularists and non-Muslims and establishing worldwide fundamentalist Islamic rule. Al Qaeda helped to fund and organize the 1993 bombing at the World Trade Center in New York City.

Because the Taliban and Osama bin Laden's Al Qaeda organization shared a commitment to *Jihad*, the Taliban invited Al Qaeda to turn Afghanistan into a base for training fighters pledged to further attacks on the United States, Israel, and moderate Muslim states. Osama bin Laden and the Taliban leader Mullah Omar forged a close alliance. Bin Laden brought his family to Afghanistan, and he and Mullah Omar even arranged marriages between their families.

From their training camps in the remote Afghan countryside, Al Qaeda organized attacks on a U.S. military apartment building in Saudi Arabia, on the U.S. embassies in Kenya and Tanzania, and on the U.S. Navy ship *Cole* in Yemen. Hundreds of people were killed in these bombings.

In Kabul, the Taliban turned Meena's former high school Malalai into a *madrassa*, where hundreds of boys sat reciting the Koran. Quotes from the holy book were scrawled on the walls. The building was allowed to decay. Tents were set up in the beautiful park around the school where Meena and her schoolmates had played. Hundreds more armed Talibs camped there, turning the grounds into a sea of mud. Mullah Omar and Osama bin Laden both visited the school, where they delivered speeches to the students.

The Talibs, fanatically enforcing the Koran's prohibition against all imagery of humans or animals, destroyed photographs, paintings, and statues wherever they saw them. They smashed television sets and cameras, and even destroyed childrens' dolls and stuffed animals. Mullah Omar personally went to the Kabul museum and forced the curators to take its treasures out of the display cases and storage rooms. Omar stood by as men with sledgehammers destroyed irreplaceable works of art that were the birthright of all Afghans. Fragile glass pieces, such as a graceful two-thousand-year-old turquoise-blue glass fish, were smashed under Omar's sledgehammer.

Ignoring an international outpouring of anguish, the Taliban blew up the tallest statues of Buddha in the world, which had been carved into a sandstone cliff in Bamiyan, Afghanistan, in the third century B.C. Afghans all over the world sent messages to the Taliban, begging them to spare their precious heritage, but in March 2001, the Talibs methodically detonated explosives day after day until the Buddhas were turned into dust.

Meena's prediction that life under the fundamentalists would be even worse than life under the Soviets came true. No group of feminists in history had ever been so challenged as RAWA was under the Taliban's rule. Even Meena could not have imagined the Taliban and Al Qaeda. Nevertheless, the example of her bravery inspired the women of RAWA to resist. They refused to give in to despair during Afghanistan's darkest years. Carefully, they had built their networks to more than two thousand members, with many thousands of supporters. They alone kept alive, for many Afghans, a flickering flame of freedom.

On the ocassion of fourth martyr

Children of RAWA's Watan (Homeland) School sing songs for Meena on the fourth anniversary of her death on February 4, 1991, in Quetta, Pakistan.

Throughout the Taliban's rule, RAWA managed to publish *Payam-e-Zan* in Pakistan. The press in Pakistan is unrestricted, and RAWA had no trouble finding sympathetic printers to help with production. RAWA's supporters, many of them in Europe, subscribed to *Payam-e-Zan* and sent funds with which RAWA also produced a more easily concealed, smaller version of the magazine, which the women, having become expert smugglers, carried into Afghanistan. *Payam-e-Zan* boldly condemned the Taliban, published photos of their atrocities and articles about acts of resistance against them.

Meena had said, "I want to let the outside world know that Afghan women aren't silent, that we struggle for the betterment of our lives."

A group of young RAWA members learned to speak English and became RAWA's ambassadors to the world. They traveled to every continent telling the story of Afghanistan's struggle.

The new generation of RAWA members made quick use of the Internet almost as soon as it came to Pakistan. In Pakistan, women are not encouraged to visit Internet shops, but a whole group of eager RAWA women became self-taught computer whizzes. In 1997, they set up RAWA's Web site (*www.rawa.org*), where visitors can view photos of Meena. When the site was set up the first words were: "Thank you for visiting the homepage of the most oppressed women in the world! If you are freedom-loving and antifundamentalist, you are with us!"

At first, only a few people visited the site each day. Then on one day in 1999, there were 300,000 visitors! The RAWA women did not know at first what had happened. Then they learned that the American TV star Oprah Winfrey had talked on her show about the situation of Afghan women under the Taliban, and RAWA's resistance.

As the only political, antifundamentalist organization of Afghan women, RAWA's nearly twenty years of experience and extensive networks of members and supporters were crucial to the survival of countless people living under the Taliban's rule.

Asifa and many other RAWA members crossed the border countless times. They brought medicines to women in need. They helped to organize clandestine schools for girls in the homes of supporters, and they brought money to help sustain the teachers.

Naheed the Tailor was one of those who sneaked into Kabul to do RAWA's work. Unused to wearing the *burqa*, she lifted hers for a moment to try to see where she was going. A Talib saw her, and attacked without warning. He knocked Naheed down, and she fell sideways, seriously injuring her back. She was left with chronic pain. She could not get surgery for such an injury in Afghanistan or Pakistan. But she still taught sewing to many destitute women.

Though they literally risked their lives and limbs to go into Afghanistan, the women of RAWA kept up their healthy spirit of defiance. They made sure that, hidden inside their shoes, their toe-nails were painted bright colors with the polish the Taliban had forbidden.

In Pakistan, RAWA held public anti-Taliban demonstrations, even in the face of threats from the Mullahs and packs of Talibs who chased them though the streets, beating them with sticks. Every year on March 8, RAWA defiantly celebrated International Women's Day with well-attended marches through the streets of Pakistani cities. In public meetings they declared their hope for achieving democracy and freedom and pledged to continue their struggle against the fundamentalists.

RAWA members were dismayed when, in May 2001, the new Bush administration in Washington sent a 43-million-dollar gift to the Taliban. Focused on the war on drugs, Secretary of State Colin Powell announced the funds were a reward for the Taliban's co-operation. The Talibs had brutally suppressed Afghan farmers who cultivated opium because the Mullahs had declared heroin was against the will of God.

RAWA used its networks to document the Taliban's dreadful human rights abuses. A brave RAWA member smuggled a video camera under her *burqa* into the crowded Kabul soccer stadium to film the execution of a mother of five children named Zarmina, accused of killing her abusive husband. The film shows a woman in a blue *burqa* being led into the center of the field. She was forced to kneel, a gun put to her head. A shot rang out, and she pitched forward into the dirt. A dark bloodstain spread over the blue cloth of her *burqa*.

RAWA smuggled the film out of Afghanistan and to the West, where it caused a furor among human rights activists and feminists. RAWA's footage was included in a BBC/CNN documentary *Behind the Veil*, released in June 2001. At last there was a small and growing movement of people who cared about Afghan women. But beyond giving much-needed funds and lobbying governments to intervene against the Taliban, there was little that concerned people could do, and most of the world was not listening.

*   *   *

On September 11, 2001, when agents of Al Qaeda hijacked airplanes and damaged the Pentagon and destroyed the World Trade Center in New York City, it was as if the collapse of the Twin Towers also brought down the veil that had shrouded Afghan women from the eyes of the world. Suddenly, their suffering under the Taliban and their two decades of war wounds were exposed for all to see. The women of RAWA knew only too well what it felt like to be persecuted by the same deadly and hateful forces that had attacked Americans. RAWA issued a statement three days after the attacks on the Twin Towers and the Pentagon. It said, "We stand with the rest of the world in expressing our sorrow and condemnation for this barbaric act of violence and terror." RAWA expressed the hope that "the great American people will be able to differentiate between the people of Afghanistan and a handful of fundamentalist terrorists. Our hearts go out to the people of the U.S."

Afghan women and RAWA suddenly came to the attention of the world. The BBC/CNN documentary *Behind the Veil*, with RAWA's footage of Zarmina's execution, was shown again and again on worldwide TV. It was a painful irony to the women of RAWA that their situation could only come to light in the wake of another terrible tragedy.

U.S. retaliation for Al Qaeda's attacks was swift. With U.S. supplies and air strikes, the Northern Alliance quickly advanced across Afghanistan as the Taliban fled into the mountains and back into Pakistan. Both Osama bin Laden and Mullah Omar escaped capture, as did most of the Taliban leadership.

A new leader, Hamid Karzai, came to Kabul from exile in the United States and was installed as president. Unfortunately, most of his interim government was made up of people with close ties to the old warlords.

When a Grand Council, a *Loya Jirga*, met to form a new government, the same gang of murderous warlords arrived to claim a share of power. Rabbani, Dostum, Sayyaf and the rest were sitting in the front row at the meetings. They reestablished their control in the rural provinces and ruled them as before.

Gulbaddin Hekmatyar immediately returned to Afghanistan from Iran. He regrouped his forces in his old stronghold near Kandahar. In November 2001, Hekmatyar directed his commanders, many of whom had been holding sway over refugee camps in Pakistan, to return to Afghanistan and to reestablish the control of his party, *Hezb-e-Islami*, over the Kandahar region. Hekmatyar later issued a public invitation in Peshawar to his old rivals, the Taliban and Al Qaeda, to come back and join him in an effort to undermine the interim government of Hamid Karzai and to fight the Americans. U.S. forces attempted to kill Hekmatyar in a missile attack in the summer of 2002, but narrowly missed him.

The members of RAWA, like the majority of the Afghan people, rejoiced to see the Taliban go, but greeted the return of the warlords with deep distrust. RAWA openly called for their arrest and trial for war crimes. The new, interim government in Afghanistan was not yet the peace and democracy for which RAWA had fought for twenty-five years. Still, RAWA gave President Karzai their cautious support, and many of its members returned to Afghanistan to help with resettling refugees and organizing relief for the victims of famine and earthquakes as well as the war.

Today, Meena's image is displayed wherever RAWA women are working. Her framed photo hangs in the front of RAWA classrooms and in doctors' offices in RAWA clinics. Her calm eyes gaze down on women's demonstrations from the picket signs they hold aloft. Her photo, sometimes just a clipping from a RAWA magazine taped to the wall, is the only adornment in many refugee camp homes. Among the thousands of Afghan victims of twenty-three years of war, she is the only widely known woman.

After September 11, RAWA was given enough funds by U.S., European, Australian, and Japanese supporters, to reopen Malalai Hospital. A committee of RAWA members found a suitable building near the Afghan refugee community outside of Islamabad, Pakistan. Two Afghan doctors came from Afghanistan to run the hospital.

Nurses volunteered their time. Several RAWA members in their early twenties took charge of remodeling the building and ordering all of the equipment, repeating the work Meena had done fifteen years before, in the last months of her life. On the day the new Malalai Hospital opened, women and children who needed treatment crowded inside. Twenty-four in-patient beds were quickly filled. Meena's framed photo smiles down on all the activity. The nurses laugh about the fact that the first nine babies born in RAWA's hospital were girls.

On February 4, 2002, hundreds of people, most of them Afghan women and girls, gathered in a large hall in Peshawar, Pakistan, to remember Meena on the fifteenth anniversary of her death. Teenagers from RAWA's high schools performed songs. A young woman read a new poem written for the occasion by an Indian-American woman, Neesha Mirchandani:

Meena Lives Within Us

MEENA: She is the beacon of hope within us
She shines the lantern into the darkness
She is the part of us that knows tomorrow will be
    better,
if we continue the struggle and spread the light.
She is the part of us that never gives up.
She is in every RAWA action, every RAWA web page,
    every media interview,
in every blanket distribution in every refugee camp,
in every school and every orphanage from Islamabad
    to Khandahar.
If the light of hope is in your heart, Meena is still
    alive.

MEENA: She is the voice of courage within us
She is not afraid of the power of the powerful
She is the part of us that speaks up with courage
She is the part of us that dispels the sea of despair

and speaks without fear to the powerful ones.
She is at RAWA's demonstrations in Islamabad
She is in the stadium in Kabul while you're filming
　Zarmina
She is there when you travel to strange lands to tell
　your story.
If your voice of courage can still be heard, Meena is
　still in this world.

MEENA: She is the source of power within us
She is not ashamed to be a strong woman
She is the part of us that believes that women de-
　serve equality
She is the part of us that refuses anything less.
And claims her human rights without apologies
Every time a woman stands up in America, in Asia,
　in Africa,
Every time RAWA protects a woman's rights,
Every time a new girl enters a RAWA school
Wherever there is a women's movement,
Meena is marching right beside them.

MEENA: She is the beauty within us.
They murdered her beautiful body
But they couldn't silence Meena's voice
They couldn't take Meena's courage
They couldn't kill Meena's hope
They couldn't steal Meena's dream
Meena is in every RAWA member
in every RAWA song
She will never die as long as we believe in her vision
Meena lives eternally within us forevermore.

In the audience that day were widows, mothers who had lost children, and many people who had lost their homes and all of their possessions. Many Afghans who cannot allow themselves to break down and weep for their own overwhelming sorrows wipe away tears when they speak of Meena. Her sacrifice stands for all of their losses.

*   *   *

EPILOGUE

• • • Almost as soon as the Taliban fled, a French nonprofit agency, ACTED, sent a team to Kabul to restore Meena's old school, Lycée Malalai. The construction was led by an Afghan woman civil engineer who had not been allowed to work for six years. She supervised a crew of two hundred Afghan men, who repaired and painted the buildings and cleaned the grounds. As many of the former teachers as could be found were rehired. On the first day of school, hundreds of girls filled the classrooms and the park once again with the happy sound of their voices.

• • • Roya and her family fled the the bombs falling on Kabul when the American attack on the Taliban began, and made their way to a RAWA-run refugee camp in Pakistan. The Taliban's end came in the nick of time for them.

Roya's husband had been selling vegetables in Kabul with the help of their young daughter, disguised in boy's clothing. One day a Talib had accosted the little girl. The Talib grabbed her and began to feel her body, demanding to know, "Are you a boy or a girl?" Roya's husband pushed and hit the Talib, trying to pull his daughter away from him. In the melee, he broke the Talib's tooth.

"You martyred my tooth!" the Talib yelled. Everyone who heard this in the crowded marketplace burst out laughing. But to the Talib, it was no laughing matter. He took Roya's husband to jail. When the Americans entered Kabul, Roya's husband was waiting

RAWA demonstration in Peshawar, Pakistan, to condemn the
1992 taking of Kabul by fundamentalist criminals.
This demonstration, held on the sixth anniversay,
April 28, 1998, was attacked by the Taliban.

A class for refugee children in the Haripur refugee camp,
Pakistan, 2001.

RAWA demonstration in Islamabad, Pakistan, on December 10,
2001, demanding democracy in Afghanistan. This demonstration
was attacked by Pakistani, Afghan, and Kashmiri fundamentalists.
Some RAWA members were injured, and others were jailed by the
Pakistani government.

to be tried, and possibly sentenced to having his hand chopped off.
But when the Americans came, the Talib guards abandoned the
prison, and the prisoners freed themselves.

"The Talibs didn't last long enough to punish my husband!"
Roya exulted. Her lined face creased even more in a joyful smile.

"I hope we can go back home, and that my husband can teach
again, and I pray the fundamentalists don't come back," she said.
"My daughter is taking karate lessons now from RAWA to fight the
Taliban if they do return. She says she would rather marry a dog
than a Talib. If there were ten more women like Meena, Afghanistan
would be rebuilt."

• • •   Asifa, Sadaf, and Basera the midwife are now senior leaders
of RAWA, working with dozens of others to oversee its health, social
welfare, and education programs in Pakistan and Afghanistan.

"Meena's dreams are not yet realized," Asifa said. "She stood for social justice for women and everyone, for democracy and freedom for our country. We still have the long-range view Meena taught us. We will always work for her ideals."

• • • The case of Meena's murder has been resolved. Over the years, RAWA had sent several delegations of members to the Machh Prison in Pakistan to question the men who had killed Meena, hoping to learn more about how she died. The women wanted nothing from the killers but to know Meena's last words. Though the women begged the men to tell them the truth, each time, they refused to talk.

Everything changed in the spring of 2002. The U.S. war in Afghanistan sent numerous Taliban and Al Qaeda fighters fleeing back into Pakistan, pursued by U.S. forces. The U.S. government put tremendous pressure on the government of Pakistan president Perez Musharref to crack down on Islamic militants. World attention was focused on the plight of Afghan women. The case of Meena's killers, which had languished, became an embarrassment to Pakistan. Acting quickly, the Pakistani government hanged Ahmed Sultan and Mohammed Hamayoun inside a prison in Baluchistan, Pakistan, on May 4, 2002. With them died the knowledge of what happened in Meena's last hours. RAWA's statement said, in part:

> RAWA opposes capital punishment. We aspire to a society where there can be no criminals of the ilk of Ahmed Sultan and Hamayoun, and hence no need for any capital punishment. We are aware, however, that we have a long, long way to go until such a society is built in Afghanistan.

Meena's sister, who had been married to Ahmed Sultan, remained living in seclusion.

• • • Meena's three children have grown safely to young adulthood with loving foster parents. Meena's daughters have followed in the path of their mother. However, her son, who was raised in the West

RAWA members distribute blankets to refugees in Masryal area
of Rawalpindi, Pakistan, January 2001.

Function in a RAWA school in Rawalpindi, May 2002.

Opening ceremony for a RAWA school for girls in a remote village of Farah province in Western Afghanistan, August, 2002.

by his foster parents, has not yet been in contact with his sisters. The identities of Meena's children are closely protected because of threats to their lives. They know they are among the luckiest of Afghanistan's many orphans.

• • • Naheed the Tailor is retired now, too disabled by her injured back to work at sewing. But she remains close to RAWA. "Today, I still feel there's a void in the world without Meena. She was so strong. I still miss her and look to her example. Meena didn't just belong to RAWA, but to all women of many countries."

• • • Mowaish, who raised Meena's oldest daughter to adulthood, is a strong and wiry grandmother now. Everyone in RAWA honors her and calls her "Dear Aunt." She said, "I used to pray every day for Meena. I still pray every day for her, but now I also pray for all of these beautiful girls of RAWA and the work they are doing."

• • • Shafika, the little girl whose long hair Meena had admired, graduated from one of RAWA's high schools in Pakistan, and then went to work for RAWA. She spent two years underground in Afghanistan under the Taliban. She had a narrow escape in Kabul when she was searched by some Talibs. Luckily, she had forgotten

RAWA school for girls in Kunar Province in Afghanistan,
October 2002.

the copies of *Payam-e-Zan* she was supposed to be carrying. If she
had had them, she could have lost her hands or even her head,
because the Taliban had openly announced that is what they would
do to anyone with such literature. Shafika is now in charge of
RAWA's medical program in one province of Pakistan. In the spring
of 2002, some extremist men broke into one of RAWA's clinics and
ransacked it. When Shafika came to inspect the damage, they threw
rocks at her, chased her away, and warned her not to come back.
She vowed to return, however.

"I'm a daughter of Meena," she said. "I try to learn from her
example. She didn't disdain minor tasks. She would type or clean
the kitchen. She never used the word 'tired,' and always had a smile
for us children."

Shafika still has beautiful long brown hair, and often, she lets
her thick shiny ponytail swing free.

AUTHOR'S NOTE

Searching for Meena

In the weeks following the attacks on America in September 2001, like many other Americans, I was awakened to the plight of the Afghan people.

I discovered RAWA's Web site and there I first saw Meena's lovely face and read about her life. From the first moment I saw her image, Meena fascinated me. When I found there was no biography of her, my literary agent, Ann Rittenberg, suggested I write one. On the phone from her Manhattan office, Ann urged, "Writers are so important at a time like this. They are like messengers, running ahead of everyone else. Writing now is a sacred duty."

I think anyone who has ever suddenly left her everyday world behind and set out for a place she has never been, to do something she has never done before, motivated by a purpose far beyond her usual life, will understand. I simply set my feet upon the path I chose. Once I started, I determinedly went forward toward this book, with a feeling of knowing where to go next.

In November 2001, "Tameena Faryal," a RAWA spokeswoman, toured the United States, using a pseudonym to shield her from possible attacks when she returned to Pakistan and Afghanistan. I wrote a brief proposal for this book and took it with me to a luncheon in Tameena's honor, hoping to meet her. I filled my plate at the buffet and looked around the crowded room, seeing no one I knew. I sat down next to a young Afghan-American woman who wore her fine, silky brown hair in a style that curved around her pretty face. She introduced herself as Latifa Popal, and said she had left Afghanistan as a teenager in 1986.

Over that lunch, Latifa told me her remarkable story: She was born in Kabul and educated there. At the age of seventeen, she had walked out of Afghanistan with her family in winter, carrying the few belongings they could pack onto donkeys, over the snowy mountains of Tora Bora to a refugee camp in Quetta, Pakistan. From there, they had migrated to Peshawar, Pakistan, where Latifa, who had graduated from high school in Kabul, taught children to read in a refugee camp. Eventually Latifa's family made their way to Norway, and then to the U.S. For the first few years, Latifa was the family's only breadwinner, as her siblings were too young to work, and her parents could not speak English. She worked two jobs: at a fast-food restaurant, and a night shift at a convalescent hospital, and put herself through college, all the while grieving for the homeland of her birth as it succumbed to war, chaos, and then the rule of the Taliban. Sadly, Latifa's father, displaced and disheartened, had died, never again to see his nation at peace.

When I told Latifa of my hope to write the first-ever biography of Meena, her first words were: "I will help you." I had no idea then how true her words would prove to be.

After Tameena Faryal's speech, I approached her, spoke to her briefly, and handed her my proposal. Tameena said, "It has always been our dream to have such a book."

It was my dream to build a bridge to Afghan women that would help American women and men to ally with them against ignorance, misogyny, and violence. The only face the world associated with Afghanistan was the bearded image of Osama bin Laden, a symbol of the Afghans' subjugation. I wanted people to also recognize Meena's face as a symbol of Afghans' love of freedom.

I have worked for more than twenty years as a private investigator, helping to prepare appeals for death row inmates. But Meena's book took precedence over everything else. As the U.S. attack on the Taliban advanced, many of my friends and I struggled to find something we could do to help innocent Afghans caught in the cross fire. Women seemed to hold the keys to positive change in Afghanistan. We saw that their demands for education, health, and freedom could bring a better world for everyone. Suddenly the situation of Afghan women meant everything to us: Their futures, we realized, could not be more closely tied to the futures of our own children and grandchildren and our hopes for all of those futures to be bearable.

Again and again, I returned to RAWA's Web site to gaze at Meena's picture. I knew Meena was an icon and a symbol to thousands of women. I longed to know her better, and hoped to create a portrait of her that would bring her to life as a complex human being.

Meena's story belongs to RAWA. I knew I would not do the book without their cooperation. I also decided from the beginning to donate any author's royalties to aid RAWA's medical and educational projects.

On November 16, an e-mail answer to my proposal came from RAWA:

> First, let us convey our deepest regards for you and the responsibility you are going to take in order to compile a book about our founding leader, Meena. We are much excited to hear about your suggestion and wholeheartedly support your efforts for completing the book as soon as possible. We also agree with the objectives you want to fulfill through the book. So we accept your proposal and want to help you in whatever way possible. Waiting to hear from you soon, Mehmooda.

I had long since learned as an investigator that nothing can substitute for face-to-face interviews with witnesses. I knew I would need to go to Afghanistan and Pakistan and talk to the people who had been close to Meena.

Working day and night, I did preliminary research and completed a proposal for Ann Rittenberg to send to publishers.

By early December, Tameena Faryal had finished her tour and was about to leave the United States and return to Pakistan and Afghanistan. I wanted to see her again, to forge a personal bond that could stretch halfway around the world and endure as together we shaped Meena's book. With no guarantee that the book would ever be a reality, I flew to Detroit.

At the home of Tameena's hostess, Azad, and Azad's daughter, Iman, I first entered the world of Afghan-American immigrants, and experienced the warmth of Afghan hospitality. Azad was the first of many many Afghan widows I was to meet; hers the first of countless stories of loss and flight from war I was to hear. She showed me a photo of her husband, a handsome young man who had been executed by the former pro-Soviet puppet government of Afghanistan. When I expressed my sorrow for her loss, Azad simply turned her head, and said, "Mine is no more than so many others' pain."

Tameena and I talked about Meena for hours over a huge lunch prepared by Azad and Iman: heaps of rice and chicken, flat Afghan bread, salad and spinach and eggplant. Tameena assumed that I would come to Pakistan and Afghanistan to interview the people who had known Meena. She answered many of my questions by saying, that when I met Meena's teacher, or her best friend, "She will tell you."

Ann Rittenberg, meanwhile, got the book proposal to the right people in New York. St. Martin's Press is located in the historic Flatiron Building on Fifth Avenue, from whose windows on September 11 people watched everything happen. Diane Higgins, a senior editor at St. Martin's, felt as Ann and I did: that the amazing story of Afghanistan's leading feminist and democrat must reach girls and women everywhere. On January 16, 2002, the contract for Meena's book was signed. We were an all-women team; American women, preparing a gift for Afghan women.

In January, I organized my journey, planning it for the first week in March and the first celebration of Women's Day in Kabul. I applied for a visa to Pakistan, from where I hoped to be able to reach Kabul, feeling very apprehensive about going alone to a place where I did not speak the languages and I knew no one. On January

23, *Wall Street Journal* reporter Daniel Pearl was kidnapped in Karachi, Pakistan.

Discussing my fears about the trip on the phone with Latifa Popal, she suddenly said, "I will go with you." I had to ask her to say it again. It was such a wonderful offer, that I was not certain I had heard her correctly. Besides her excellent English, Latifa speaks Farsi, Dari, Pashtu, some Urdu, and even Spanish. Our journey to Kabul was to be Latifa's homecoming. For the first time in seventeen years, she would set foot in her home country, and see the city of her childhood.

On February 24, after the news had come that Daniel Pearl had been murdered, his wife, Marianne Pearl, wrote: ". . . We need to overcome cultural and religious differences. . . . We are all going to need courage and commitment. Let us inspire each other to goodness."

With those words encouraging us, we boarded an aging and jam-packed Pakistan International Airlines 747 in New York, already exhausted from the rush to get visas, tickets, immunizations, and raise the money for the trip. Our bags were heavy with gifts for Latifa's relatives. Thirty hours later, we were in the crowded airport in Rawalpindi, feeling conspicuous among the throngs of pilgrims returning from making the Haj to Mecca.

We put on the *chadors* Latifa's mother had stitched for us and made our way to a small guesthouse in Islamabad, where the owner took us in like members of his family. At the end of the terrace near our room, an armed guard stood watch.

Meena was famous for her punctuality, a trait all of RAWA has apparently adopted. The next morning, our RAWA contact showed up just as promised. She was the first of a half dozen young English-speaking women we met who serve as liaisons to RAWA's foreign visitors.

We began our work right away. We never saw the tourist sites of Pakistan, because we had such a long list of women to interview. We met the women who had known Meena, sitting with them over cups of tea in hotel rooms and in private homes in Islamabad, Rawalpindi, and Peshawar, and in rural and urban refugee camps. We talked to twenty-two RAWA members altogether, some of whom had known Meena during most of her life. We met many more people close to RAWA, such as the amazing "male support-ers"—some of them veterans of the war against the Soviets—who support the aims of RAWA and work long hours to further them. We toured RAWA's hospital and one of their orphanages and met staff members who paused in their work to talk to us. Everywhere we went, we saw Meena's portrait; sometimes in a frame, behind a doctor busy examining sick children, sometimes pinned up, the only decoration in a simple home.

We met mothers who had fled their country and were raising their children in refugee camps, without the barest necessities—without adequate food, clean water, or incomes. Yet they worked ceaselessly to help one another, teaching school, volunteering at RAWA's hospital, giving orphans loving care. RAWA members are amazingly diverse: We met young and old members, well-educated women and illiterate women, grandmothers and young unmarried girls. We met Pashtuns and Tajiks, middle-class doctors and landless peasants. We met young women who were going to school full-time and at night answering e-mails, raising funds, adminis-tering programs. We wondered when they ever slept! They found time somehow to make complex arrangements for us every day, taking care of our safety above all else.

When I first read RAWA's Web site, it said, "Welcome to the Web site of the most oppressed women in the world." They are also among the bravest women in the world. The women of RAWA have to take constant security precautions, never letting anyone learn their real names or where they live.

Latifa turned out to be a gifted translator. She is a good listener, and she conveyed the feeling as well as the content of the speakers' words, erasing the language barrier between us as we sat huddled for hours, seated on the floor, or on the edges of hotel-room beds, talking and listening and talking some more.

The women of RAWA took me in with an immediate and generous love. They enfolded me in long hugs, and again and again kissed my face and my hands. There can be no more humbling experience for a writer than to be kissed and thanked by an illiterate woman for writing a book that she will not be able to read.

We never met an Afghan man or woman whose family was intact. Everyone we met had lost family members in Afghanistan's two decades of war. Sometimes as they talked of their losses, they did not cry, and it seemed as though to do so would be to open up too much to the pain. Our eyes, however, brimmed over. Our *chadors*, which we found so cumbersome to wear, at least proved handy for wiping away tears. Every woman we interviewed seemed to minimize her own suffering. Every one of them, as Azad had done in Detroit, brushed aside condolences saying, "My loss is less than many other people's losses." At first, I did not understand this. In America, our habit so often is to raise our own suffering up as unique. I came to understand that in the face of a whole nation's disaster, to separate one's own pain from the rest is to feel alone, which would be too much to bear. Comfort lies in staying closely tied to everyone else who is also dispossessed, weary, and grieving.

When the women we met spoke of Meena, their eyes shone as they talked of how she inspired them, and how her example kept them going. And every one of them wept when they talked about her death at such a young age. I realized that for them, Meena is the container for all of the pain of the losses they have suffered. If they cannot cry for themselves, they can cry for Meena.

One way perhaps to convey to Americans what Meena means to Afghans is to say that to them she is their Rosa Parks: Her brave and unprecedented action went far beyond her own life and will always be honored. She was their Harriet Tubman, journeying back into danger over and over again to lead others to safety. She was their Susan B. Anthony: She had a vision of what women could accomplish that they will never stop striving to achieve.

We flew from Islamabad to Kabul on March 6, aboard a United

Nations plane. Before we even landed, the sight of wrecked tanks and planes and blasted houses all around the airport stripped away from Latifa all memories of her formerly beautiful home city. As we entered Kabul, Latifa stared around her with disbelief at the destruction. She remembered broad avenues with flowers and big modern electric buses. We saw only mud, broken pavement, and, as soon as we got out of the World Food Program van that gave us a ride into the city, broken children. We were instantly surrounded by youngsters who had been hurt by land mines, hobbling on crude crutches and begging for food. As they gathered around Latifa to answer her questions, I saw that many of them had startling light green eyes and silky fine hair like hers.

We passed by Latifa's own high school, destroyed. Gazing out the car window, looking utterly bereft, she said, "I will not go there. I cannot see my school like that." She went into a state of shock that has not completely left her; it was the pain of a refugee who realizes that she can never go back home, because the home she knew no longer exists.

After difficulties with phones and cars and directions, we found Latifa's favorite cousin, a warm and loving father, a moderate Muslim who loves the poems of Jelaluddin Balkhi, known in the West as Rumi. Latifa's cousin and his family had refused to leave their homeland, and had endured in poverty through the years of war and Taliban rule. They had heard news through a secret radio a friend had kept even during the Taliban. When the American bombing began, they had cowered with their children in the basement of their apartment building as bombs fell close by, killing some of their neighbors.

Latifa's cousin's wife, a teacher, had been forced by the Taliban to leave her job and to stay indoors for six years, tutoring their daughters. Already, she had returned to work, and the depression she had suffered during her confinement had lifted.

We made contact with the important RAWA member we had come to meet. This sensitive and educated woman had been at Meena's side at many of the most difficult moments of her life. A senior leader, and veteran of more than twenty years in RAWA, she arrived and left hidden under a *burqa*. Though the Taliban had fled Kabul, RAWA then, as now, was unwilling to expose their identities, because the former warlords had resumed power—men who are hardly less of a danger to the human rights of women and men than the Taliban leaders. One of RAWA's important functions has always been to warn of danger. Meena had warned as early as 1981 of the danger of the extremists. No one knows better than RAWA the threat they continue to pose to Afghan liberty today.

We attended the Women's Day celebration inside the bombed shell of a movie theater. The building's roof had been blown away, and a huge red-and-white tent, normally used for wedding celebrations, had been stretched over the crumbling walls to serve as a ceiling. The hall was guarded by International Peace Keepers in their light blue U.N. insignia. The Afghan women's excitement and joy to be free of the Taliban was unmistakable. We listened to Hamid Karzai, soon to be chosen interim president, and to Mary Robinson, the United Nations High Commissioner for Human Rights. She stressed that human rights had to be guaranteed in Afghanistan from the beginning; had to come along with the needed food and security, not as an afterthought. Many hopeful words about Afghan women were spoken, but it was plain that their future was uncertain. At the end of the speeches, a little girl in a traditional dress embroidered in red opened a birdcage to free two doves as a symbol of peace. One white dove flew right up and perched in a high niche in the crumbing brick wall. But the other dove cowered inside the cage and refused to come out. It was the perfect expression of the hopes of Afghan women, but also their fears.

Kabul was a thousand paradoxes: our hotel, which had no running water and only sporadic electricity, housed both dozens of women who had arrived from all over Afghanistan for Women's Day, and a group of armed-to-the-teeth war lords, who had come to the capital for a conference with the government. The hotel staff told us that for years, there had been no foreign guests, and that only Al Queda leaders had stayed in that hotel, including Osama bin Laden. The friendly young men at the reception desk seemed understandably confused—both delighted and disturbed by the sight of unveiled women walking around the lobby. We teased them. "Welcome home!" I said. "You've been to the Planet of No Women. Welcome back to Earth, where women are half of the people!" They laughed, as a French journalist smiled and quipped, "Give them time, they will be all right." Later, I heard him trying to convince them that it would even be okay to have a woman boss.

When we visited Meena's high school, we walked where we knew she had walked, and we felt her spirit, alive in the men and women who were working so hard to restore a place where girls could learn. We stood for a few minutes under the trees, imagining that one day perhaps a monument to Meena's memory could be placed there.

There were no seats for us on the return flight to Islamabad, so Latifa's cousins arranged a car, a driver, and a bodyguard for us to return to Pakistan over the Khyber Pass. After five days in Kabul Latifa said good-bye to her family there, hoping she would be able to return.

Our car headed east from Kabul on a narrow, rutted road. Fighting was still going on in the mountains, and we saw newly formed camps of people who had been displaced by the U.S. bombing campaign. But most people we saw on the road were traveling in the opposite direction. The whole way to the border our car dodged a stream of brightly decorated Pakistani trucks, each one packed with Afghans returning from refugee camps in Pakistan. Families were pressed tightly together, standing up in the backs of the open-air trucks, rushing back into their homeland. Each family, we were told, had been given five dollars per person, a plastic bucket, and a bag of rice. With these few poor possessions, thousands of Afghans were returning to take their chances, hoping to reestablish life in their own nation.

Afghanistan is so beautiful, it is easy to understand why its people want to go home to it. We drove through a steep river canyon, high above a tumultuous river. As the road descended, we saw bright green terraced fields, and small villages where farmers pulled plows and grazed goats under snowy peaks in the distance. We crossed desert oases where nomads camped with their camels. I felt so fortunate to have the chance to see some of Afghanistan, a place of so much beauty that it seemed impossible for it to have anything at all to do with war. One day soon, I hope it will be the peaceful jewel of this world, a place many people can visit and admire.

Hundreds of Americans who share my fervent hope for a peaceful Afghanistan contributed to the making of this book. I would like to especially thank my agent, the brilliant Ann Rittenberg, whose imagination conceived this book and whose steady hand guided it. The manuscript benefited from editorial suggestions from my talented friends, Susan Moon, Barbara Selfridge, Karen Payne, Arlene Blum, Jan Sells, and Dina Dubois. I received invaluable advice from Canadian anthropologist Dale Chandler and American sociologist Dr. Anne Brodsky. I am indebted to Parisian Armelle Chervel for research on Meena's visit to France. Melanie Phoenix contributed hours at her keyboard. Every person at St. Martin's Press who touched this project, especially the incomparable Nichole Argyres, worked to make a beautiful book for Meena. We all labored out of love for our Afghan sisters.

Our journey to Afghanistan was difficult to arrange and very expensive. With the help of the Buddhist Peace Fellowship, which adopted Meena's book project as one of the organization's peacemaking efforts, in just a few weeks we raised the funds Latifa Popal and I needed. As is so often true, few of our hundreds of donors were people with wealth; most were ordinary working Americans, all with goodwill toward the Afghan people and Islam's peaceful tradition. Fund-raising events were organized for us by Sandy Hunter, Gordon and Margo Tyndall, and Patrice Wynne. Incredible feats of last-minute fund-raising were achieved by Jeanne Friedman and Pamela Krasney. Sadly, Judith Stronach, who gave us so much encouragement, did not live to see the book completed, but her work for peace will long outlive her.

This book is a gift from American women to Afghan women, which was accomplished with the assistance of many "male supporters," chief among them Stan Dewey, my husband.

Alice Walker's moving foreword and Jane Hirshfield's sensitive and skilled work with Meena's poetry are two more heartfelt gifts from American women who wanted to help create a tribute worthy of Meena.

We brought back with us to America an indelible impression of the love Afghan women hold in their hearts for Meena. We found her alive in them, inspiring them in their struggle every day.

CHRONOLOGY

1839–42 The first Anglo-Afghan war.

1878–80 The second Anglo-Afghan war, in which the heroine Malalai raises the Afghan flag in the Battle of Maiwand.

1921 Third Anglo-Afghan war. Afghanistan is fully independent. King Amanullah begins the social and political modernization of Afghanistan. Women's education advanced.

1933–73 The reign of Western-oriented King Mohammed Zahir.

1947 British withdraw from India.
Pakistan and India are partitioned.

1953 Prince Mohammed Daoud becomes prime minister of Afghanistan under his cousin, King Zahir.

1955 Daoud goes to U.S.S.R. for aid; closer ties between Afghanistan and U.S.S.R.

1957 Meena is born in Kabul.

1959 Prime Minister Daoud and other ministers appear in public with their wives unveiled. The veil is made optional, Kabul University is opened to women.
Women enter the workforce and government.

1963 King Zahir removes Prime Minister Daoud.

1964 Women participate in writing a new democratic constitution proclaiming the vote for women.
Leonid Brezhnev becomes leader of U.S.S.R.

1965 The first national elections are held. Men and women vote.
Afghan People's Democratic Party formed.

1973 King Zahir overthrown by former prime minister Daoud and members of the pro-Soviet Afghan People's Democratic Party. The monarchy is abolished. Daoud declares himself president.

1976   Meena begins her studies at Kabul University, and marries.

1977   Meena founds RAWA.

1978   April: pro-Soviet political party carries out a coup and assassinates Daoud. Thousands of Afghan intellectuals and democrats are imprisoned or killed.

1979   February: The U.S. Ambassador is kidnapped and murdered.
New regime signs treaty with the U.S.S.R.
Two Afghan presidents killed in succession.
December: Soviet troops invade Afghanistan.

1979–80   The Iranian revolution brings Ayatollah Khomeini to power.
U.S. hostages held in Teheran.

1980   *Mujahedeen*, anticommunist, Islamic rebels begin war against the Soviet occupiers of Afghanistan.
Massive anti-Soviet student demonstrations in Kabul.
RAWA's magazine, *Payam-e-Zan* founded.

1981   Meena travels to Europe representing RAWA.
Fundamentalists assassinate Sadat in Egypt.

1982   Meena returns to Kabul, then takes refuge in Pakistan.
Osama bin Laden moves to Pakistan.
Andropov becomes leader of U.S.S.R.

1982–86   Meena leads RAWA to found schools, workshops, orphanages, and Malalai Hospital in Pakistan. She travels undercover into Afghanistan numerous times to lead RAWA activities there.

1986   February: Soviet reform leader Gorbachev calls Afghanistan "a bleeding wound."

1987   February 4: Meena disappears.
Mujahedeen make great gains.
RAWA reorganizes, carries on work in aid of refugees and war victims inside Afghanistan.

1989	February: Soviet troops concede defeat, withdraw from Afghanistan, leaving the puppet Najibullah regime in power. The *mujahedeen* fight on against Najibullah.
1992	April: *Mujahedeen* take Kabul, overthrow Najibullah.
1993	Civil war between Rabbani, Dostum, and Hekmatyar kills tens of thousands.
1994	The civil war reduces Kabul to ruins. The Taliban forms in Pakistan.
1995	November: Taliban conquer Kandahar. September: Taliban conquer Herat.
1996	September: Taliban conquer Kabul. Osama bin Laden establishes Al Queda camps in Afghanistan.
1998	August: Al Queda bombs U.S. embassies in Kenya and Tanzania.
2001	March: Taliban blow up the world's largest standing Buddha statues at Bamiyan, Afghanistan. September 11: Four airplanes hijacked by Al Queda crash in Pennsylvania, damage the Pentagon, and destroy the World Trade Center in New York. October: U.S. and Britain conduct bombing offensive in Afghanistan against Taliban and Al Queda. November: Northern Alliance conquers Kabul.
2002	Fifteenth commemoration of Meena's death held in Peshawar, Pakistan. March: First Women's Day celebration in Kabul.

FURTHER READING

On RAWA:

BENARD, Cheryl, *Veiled Courage: Inside the Afghan Women's Resistance* (Broadway Books, New York, 2002). A popular history of RAWA's role in-Afghanistan.

BRODSKY, A. E., *With All Our Strength: The Revolutionary Association of the Women of Afghanistan* (Routledge, New York, 2003). An in-depth sociological and historical study of RAWA.

On Afghanistan and the Taliban:

ANSARY, Tamin, *West of Kabul, East of New York: An Afghan-American Story* (Farrar, Straus & Giroux, 2002). An Afghan-American's loving memories of the country of his birth.

ELLIS, Deborah, *The Breadwinner* (Groundwood Books, Toronto, 2000). The compelling story, written for young readers, of a girl who passed as a boy in order to support her family during the rule of the Taliban.

RASHID, Ahmed, *Taliban* (Yale Nota Bene, 2001). A history of the Taliban movement.

On Women and Islam:

EL SAADAWI, Nawal, *Walking Through Fire: A Life of Nawal El Saadawi* (ZED Books, 2002). The inspiring autobiography of Egypt's leading feminist scholar and author.

FERNEA, Elizabeth Warnock, *Guests of the Sheik: An Ethnography of an Iraqi Village* (Doubleday Anchor, New York, 1969). An American woman's account of her life among her women friends in Iraq.

NASRIN, Taslima, *Meyebela: My Bengali Girlhood: A Memoir of Growing up Female in a Muslim World* (Steer Forth Press, Vermont, 1998). The memories of a renowned feminist and dissident driven into exile.

BROOKS, Geraldine, *Nine Parts of Desire: The Hidden World of Islamic Women* (Anchor Books, 1996). A survey of the status of women throughout the Muslim world.

ARMSTRONG, Karen, *Islam: A Short History* (Random House, New York, 2000).

And on the Poetic Tradition of Afghanistan:

BARKS, Coleman, *The Essential Rumi* (Castle Books, 1997). Translations of the poetry of Jelaluddin Balkhi.

Internet resources: www.rawa.org; www.afghanwomensmission.org.

INDEX